Pride Without Prejudice

Pride Without Prejudice

Jennifer Lang

The Story of London's Guilds & Livery Companies

with a foreword by

Sir Hugh Wontner

LONDON
Perpetua Press
1975

First published 1975
by Perpetua Press Limited
32/34 Wellington Street, London WC2

Designed by Richard Fowler and Robin Ellis
Endpaper map by William Bromage
Printed and bound in France
by Maury-Imprimeur SA
and André Brun
45330 Malesherbes

Acknowledgements

There are a great many people without whose kindness, help and advice this book could never have been written. First of all I should like to thank the Livery Companies themselves, whose clerks, beadles, archivists and librarians have given me so much of their time, as well as free access to their Companies' histories. The Clerks of the Great Twelve Companies deserve special thanks for their perseverance in checking the final manuscript and hunting down errata. I would also like to thank the staff at Guildhall; Mr. Ronnie Ryall for lending me his valuable scrap books; Alderman Ring for lending me his ancient cookery books and for the benefit of his vast experience in the history of catering and food; Sir Donald Allen, Clerk to the Trustees of London Parochial Charities until 1965, for his help with 'Charities'; and Mr. Woodbine Parish, Chairman of the City and Guilds of London Institute.

In obtaining illustrations I am very grateful to the Photography Department of The Polytechnic of Central London for allowing Mr. Robert Irons, one of their third year students, to work on the project; Mr. Howdego, Keeper of Prints and Drawings in Guildhall Library, and the individual Livery Companies, especially the Goldsmiths, who lent me so many illustrations of the Companies' plate.

Finally, I should like to thank Mr. Anthony Hignett for patient and perceptive editing; Robert Yeatman for his time, effort and attention to detail in getting the book to press; Sir Gilbert Inglefield for encouragement, support and enthusiasm from start to finish and Sir Hugh Wontner for his gracious Foreword.

For my god-daughter Nicola Haldane
whose father first suggested the idea for this book

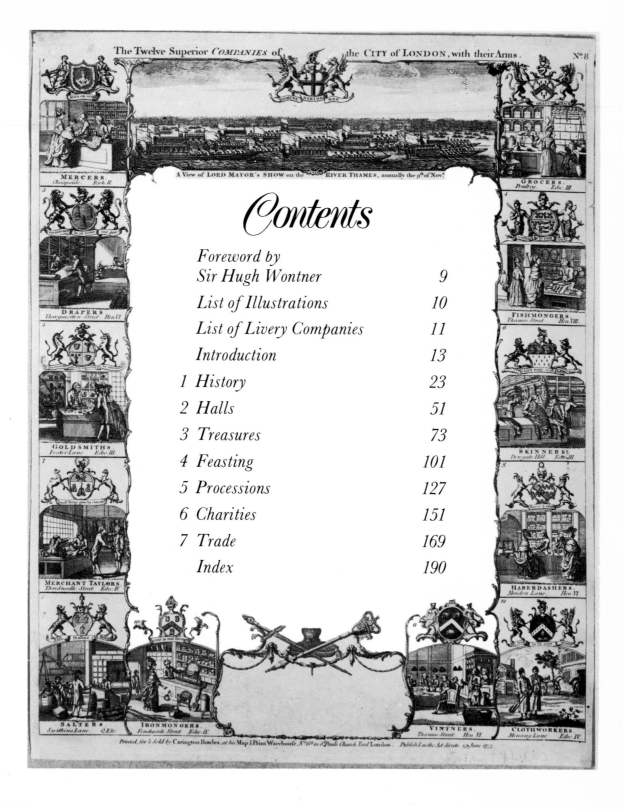

A View of LORD MAYOR's SHOW on the RIVER THAMES, annually the 9th of Nov.r

MERCERS.
Cheapside.　Rich.II.

GROCERS.
Poultry.　Edw.III.

DRAPERS.
Throgmorton Street　Hen.VI.

FISHMONGERS.
Thames Street　Hen.VIII.

GOLDSMITHS.
Foster Lane.　Edw.III.

SKINNERS.
Dowgate Hill　Edw.III.

MERCHANT TAYLORS.
Threadneedle Street　Edw.III.

HABERDASHERS.
Maiden Lane.　Hen.VI.

SALTERS.
Swithins Lane　Q.Eliz.

IRONMONGERS.
Fenchurch Street　Edw.IV.

VINTNERS.
Thames Street　Hen.VI.

CLOTHWORKERS.
Mincing Lane.　Edw.IV.

Contents

Printed, for & Sold by Carington Bowles, at his Map & Print Warehouse Nº 69 in St Pauls Church Yard, London. Published as the Act directs 25 June 1777.

Foreword

In no other city in the world is there a group of Companies, founded between the twelfth and the present century, not engaged in commerce, but each representing a different pursuit, occupation or trade, either still or originally carried on within the bounds of the City of London. Only the very new Companies, such as the Guild of Air Pilots and Air Navigators, have obviously not been connected with the City, but it is an indication of the prestige attaching to these City Companies that those engaged in entirely modern pursuits, like flying, have sought and obtained permission from the City Fathers to establish a Company similar to the others.

All these Companies are called Livery Companies because originally the members wore a livery. It is one of the remarkable features of City life that they not only exist but flourish today, and there is no more interesting subject for a book than the story of these Companies. Miss Jennifer Lang is to be congratulated on writing it with such skill and scholarship.

To tell the story of each Company, and to give an impression not only of the events of hundreds of years, but of the romance attaching to them, involves a task of selection on a huge scale. A book can be written very easily about one single Company—and, indeed, this has more than once been done—but to give a comprehensive account of so many of the Companies is a special achievement. It is my hope that those who read the story Miss Lang has written will be impressed by the astonishing survival of a medieval idea, adapted to meet the needs of such a great variety of trades and professions carried on through the country's history until the present day.

It gives me very great pleasure, as a Freeman of the City of London, a liveryman of the Worshipful Company of Feltmakers and of the Worshipful Company of Clockmakers, to write this foreword, which I am proud at the present time to be able to do as the 646th Lord Mayor of London, and the present Master of the Feltmakers' Company.

Sir Hugh Wontner

List of Illustrations

List of Livery Companies in order of Precedence

		Date of charter
1	Mercers	1393
2	Grocers	1345
3	Drapers	1364
4	Fishmongers	1364
5	Goldsmiths	1327
6	Skinners	1327
7	Merchant Taylors	1326
8	Haberdashers	1448
9	Salters	1559
10	Ironmongers	1454
11	Vintners	1437
12	Clothworkers	1528
13	Dyers	1471
14	Brewers	1437
15	Leathersellers	1444
16	Pewterers	1473
17	Barber-Surgeons	1462
18	Cutlers	1415
19	Bakers	1307
20	Wax-Chandlers	1483
21	Tallow Chandlers	1462
22	Armourers and Brasiers	1453
23	Girdlers	1448
24	Butchers	1606
25	Saddlers	1272
26	Carpenters	1477
27	Cordwainers	1438
28	Painter Stainers	1467
29	Curriers	1606
30	Masons	1677
31	Plumbers	1611
32	Innholders	1515

		Date of charter
33	Founders	1614
34	Poulterers	1504
35	Cooks	1482
36	Coopers	1501
37	Tylers and Bricklayers	1568
38	Bowyers	1621
39	Fletchers	1536
40	Blacksmiths	1571
41	Joiners and Ceilers	1571
42	Weavers	1184
43	Woolmen	1484
44	Scriveners	1617
45	Fruiterers	1606
46	Plaisterers	1501
47	Stationers and Newspaper Makers	1556
48	Broderers	1564
49	Upholders	1626
50	Musicians	1604
51	Turners	1604
52	Basketmakers	1568
53	Glaziers	1631
54	Horners	1638
55	Farriers	1684
56	Paviors	1480
57	Loriners	1712
58	Apothecaries	1606
59	Shipwrights	1605
60	Spectacle Makers	1629
61	Clockmakers	1631

		Date of charter
62	Glovers	1639
63	Feltmakers	1604
64	Framework Knitters	1657
65	Needlemakers	1656
66	Gardeners	1605
67	Tin Plate Workers	1671
68	Wheelwrights	1670
69	Distillers	1638
70	Pattenmakers	1671
71	Glass Sellers	1664
72	Coachmakers and Coach Harness Makers	1677
73	Gunmakers	1637
74	Gold and Silver Wyre Drawers	1693
75	Makers of Playing Cards	1628
76	Fanmakers	1709
77	Carmen	1656
78	Master Mariners	1929
79	Solicitors	1944
80	Farmers	1952
81	Air Pilots and Navigators	1955
82	Tobacco Pipe Makers and Tobacco Blenders	1960
83	Furniture Makers	1963
84	Scientific Instrument Makers	1964

Introduction

This Introduction is for those who do not know what Livery Companies really are; who believe them to be a relic of some sort of medieval trade union, wrapped in ermine and mysterious practices. It contains nothing which any liveryman does not already know, so that those cognizant with their inner secrets can go straight to Chapter 1, where the story of the Livery Companies' early origins begins.

Part of the mystique attached to the idea of Livery Companies is caused by the fact that it is so difficult to lay down hard and fast definitions of exactly what they are. A guild obtains its charter from the monarch, but its grant of livery since 1506 comes from the Court of Aldermen.

> They expect to be satisfied that a number of men of good repute from some trade or mystery not already represented by an existing guild have joined together as a body and have held together for a time sufficiently long to justify the belief that they will continue to hold together and are not likely to fall apart from lack of interest or support.

Definitions are vague and long-winded because for every simple rule there is always at least one Company which is an exception. For instance, there are two Ancient Guilds which still have no livery: the Parish Clerks, who received their first charter from Henry VI in 1442, never applied for a grant of livery. The Watermen and Lightermen were incorporated by Act of Parliament in 1555, and were therefore outside the jurisdiction of the Lord Mayor so were not entitled to vote for him. Many Companies did not receive a grant of livery until centuries after they had been incorporated as a guild.

Since each Company developed according to the needs of its craft they are very individualistic, although outwardly characterized by a high degree of uniformity. Some common denominators are that a Company is administered by its

A carved wood and gilt Master's chair dating from about 1681. It was given to the Framework Knitters Company by Thomas Carwarden.

governing body composed of Master, Wardens and Court of Assistants. They are elected annually from the livery and service on the Court tends to be by seniority. Some Companies have Prime Wardens instead of Masters, others have permanent honorary Grand Masters and annually elected Deputy Masters. The Guild of Air Pilots and Air Navigators, for instance, have the Duke of Edinburgh as their Grand Master and an annually elected Master. The exception even to this rule is the Cooks Company, who have two Masters. This is due to an embarrassing moment in the fifteenth century when the Master of the Cooks was summoned by the King and the Lord Mayor at exactly the same time. Since no man has ever found it possible to be in two places at once, the Cooks guarded against a repetition of this delicate question of priority by electing two Masters. One attended the reigning sovereign at the Royal Table on occasions and the other supervised the Royal Kitchen and was also available to obey any peremptory summons from the Lord Mayor. Both Masters were personally responsible for guaranteeing that neither the King nor the Queen was served with poisonous food. The Cooks Company still elects two Masters, as specified in its Charter.

Whatever his title, the Master's power and influence over his Company during his year of office is considerable. His role is also an arduous one. Many dinners have to be eaten and speeches made in the course of the year, and in addition he has to preside over Court meetings for the administration of the Company's affairs, attend City functions as the representative of his Company and support the Lord Mayor on occasions. He is not, however, entirely unprepared for the task, as he will already have spent several years on the Court of his Company and probably at least two helping his Master in the role of Warden. The number of Wardens varies from two upwards. Many Companies have a Renter Warden, who is in charge of the financial affairs of the Company—the Vintners and Dyers have an additional Swan Warden and the Butchers a Providator—whose duties correspond with those of a Steward. Their work is augmented by the Court of Assistants who vary in number from Company to Company, but the average is about twenty.

Whereas the governing body of a Company is a voluntary body, its chief executive is the Clerk, who is permanent and salaried. The nature of his duties varies according to the size and wealth of his Company. In the greatest he is backed up by Assistant Clerks, archivists, librarians, secretaries, and a bevy of paid employees; in the smallest he is a part-time servant of the Company, often trying to combine his diverse duties as Clerk with a demanding profession of his own. He needs a considerable knowledge of law, as so much of a Company's affairs are tied up with property and the charitable trust funds it administers; a gastronomic flair and a feel for history and tradition, since he has to supervise the Company's hospitality; a nice understanding of etiquette and protocol since he has to plan his Company's participation in various City functions during the year; and, finally, consummate tact to enable him to be close friend and mentor to a succession of widely differing Masters. In some Companies the job of Clerk is a very traditional one confined to one family, whereby son has succeeded father in unbroken line as far back as the eighteenth century.

A Clerk does have someone he can turn to – the Beadle, also a permanent and salaried servant of the Company. The duties of the Beadle are almost as diverse as those of his Clerk. They range from cutting a dignified and magnificent figure, begowned and bebraided in procession, to rolling up his sleeves and helping prepare a feast for the livery. If his Company has a hall, he may well be caretaker, guide and custodian. He often makes a study of the Company's past through the minute books, and his knowledge of its history and treasures may be extensive.

The main body of a Company is made up of liverymen, freemen and freewomen. There are some 25,000 freemen of the City of London of which 17,000 are liverymen. The number in each Company varies. In small family Companies like the Saddlers or the Cutlers the number of liverymen is limited to ninety, but in others like the Mercers or Drapers there are as many as two hundred. Some Companies are limited by their charters in the number they are allowed, whereas others may have as many as they choose.

Although there are still some Companies, such as the Brewers, Furniture Makers, Air Pilots and Air Navigators, Distillers, Solicitors, Stationers, Scriveners and Master Mariners, who only admit those directly involved in the trade or profession they represent, the majority of liverymen and freemen do not today personally need to have mastered the craft of the Company they seek to join. There are four different ways in which it is possible to become a freeman of a City Guild – patrimony, servitude, redemption or presentation. The last is the most difficult since it is reserved for those either whose presence in the Company would bring a great deal of prestige or who have been of great service to the Company.

Nearly every Company presents its honorary freedom to one or two people; the Royal Family, great service chiefs and elder statemen are considered good honorary material. In fact some members of the Royal Family also belong to a Livery Company by patrimony, an ancient system of hereditary privilege, by which any child who has been born after his father's admission to the freedom may take up the freedom of that Company on attaining the age of twenty-one, regardless of his trade or profession. The Queen is a freewoman of the Drapers Company by patrimony because Georve VI was a Draper before she was born; the Fishmongers Company is the Duke of Edinburgh's mother Company and both Prince Charles and Princess Anne are Fishmongers by patrimony. This system of hereditary selection was the means by which the guilds first expanded their membership, and therefore their influence, beyond the strictest limitation of their craft. It also allowed for the inclusion of women, since daughters as well as sons were permitted to exercise their hereditary rights.

Servitude involves serving an apprenticeship of between four and seven years. It was a very common method when all the members of the guilds were still practising their crafts, but nowadays, with the exception of a few Companies, the binding of apprentices is a mere formality. The Goldsmiths Company is a notable exception. They still bind apprentices in the true sense of the word. An aspiring silversmith is apprenticed for a statutory period of five years, at the end of which he submits to the Wardens of the Company his 'master-piece'. The word has come to mean a work of art of exceptional merit, but originally it only meant that it was the first piece of craftsmanship made by an apprentice entirely on his own, to prove that he had mastered his craft. Provided the master-piece is up to the required standard the apprentice is then invited to take an oath of loyalty to the Company and by doing so becomes a freeman by service and fully fledged member of his trade. Many eminent silversmiths of today were as youths bound apprentices at Goldsmiths Hall in a ceremony which has continued almost unchanged for centuries.

Redemption is a euphemism for buying the freedom of a Company, and, particularly since the eighteenth century, has been a useful and common practice. It achieves the twofold advantage of widening the base of the Company to include desirable new members unconnected with the trade and of improving its finances. It is impossible to say what it may cost to be an active member of a Livery Company, because like London clubs, this varies considerably from Company to Company. It is probably true to say that the more prestigious a Company the less it costs to be a liveryman but the more difficult it is to be elected.

Once a man, or a woman, is free of a Company the next step is to attend the Chamberlain's Court in the Guildhall, to receive the freedom of the City of London. The privileges attached to this today are insubstantial, being largely confined to an intangible feeling of fellowship and security in hard times. However, the added respectability created by the possession of a freeman's certificate has been known to be of practical help on at least one occasion. A worthy citizen and freeman of London while travelling abroad happened to fall foul of the native constabulary. Production of his passport did little to encourage them to overlook his misdemeanour, but luckily he was also carrying his freedom certificate and when he showed his captors this precious document, they immediately agreed that any freeman of the great City of London must be irreproachable.

Freedom of a Company does not lead immediately to election to the livery. Usually there is a period of waiting until a vacancy occurs and this can vary from one or two years to twenty or more. In some the livery consists only of the more senior members of the Company. A freeman pays a fine upon election to the livery and then at a simple ceremony performed by the Master and Wardens of the Company he is 'clothed' with the Company's livery. Nowadays he disrobes again almost immediately, as in most Companies only the Master and Wardens wear their gowns when engaged in the Company's business. The Painter Stainers, however, all wear their livery gowns at their annual church service and time of election.

The suits of livery from which the Companies derive their name are a relic of the feudal system. Originally 'livery' meant an allowance of food and clothing given to retainers and officers of a great household, whether of a baron, monastery, college or guild. Then the term came to be restricted to a gift of clothing and finally a uniform by which the order might be recognized. The gowns today are similar in syle to the kind worn by monks in the Middle Ages, except that they no longer have hoods. Each Company has a slightly different colour and design of gown. The Wax Chandlers recently decided to give theirs a new look and asked a well-known theatrical costumier to produce something appropriate. When they appeared arrayed in their fresh plumage at a joint guild service in St Paul's Cathedral, there was some envy and a few raised eyebrows among their brethren in other more traditionalist Companies.

Livery Companies are not, and never have been, strictly all-male preserves. In the fourteenth and fifteenth centuries when the guilds were composed of practising members of the craft, women shared in the work. The Cooks Company ordinances of 1495 refer to freemaidens, and the Drapers Company had freewomen who were on a par with the men and allowed to take apprentices and run their own businesses. They were not, however, elected to the livery and played no part in the running of the guild until present times. By the twentieth century female encroachment into trade and profession began to be reflected by a freewoman or two being elected to the livery in Companies most associated with their trades. Today, for instance, there are women doctors in the Apothecaries, women opticians in the Spectacle Makers, women pilots like Sheila Scott and Jill McKay on the livery of the Guild of Air Pilots and Air Navigators, and women lawyers in the Solicitors Company, who play an active part in Company affairs and attend livery dinners in their own right instead of just as guests on Ladies' Nights.

The inclusion of ladies among the livery creates an interesting precedent when they wish to play an active part in the administration of their Company. The Stationers and Newspaper Makers Company, for instance, already has a woman member on its Court of Assistants whose presence will pose a delicate problem a few years hence. The system of electing Masters by seniority means that inevitably her turn will come, and unless the Stationers and Newspaper Makers dodges the issue, it will be the first Livery Company ever to have a woman 'Master'.

It is not only leadership of the Livery Companies which could be affected but of the City itself. The City is governed by the Corporation of London made up of twenty-six Aldermen and 159 Common Councilmen, who are elected by the citizens. The Corporation is headed by the Lord Mayor elected by the liverymen from the twenty-six Aldermen. The process by which a man reaches the position of Lord Mayor begins therefore when he is elected an Alderman by the citizens of London. Death, disease or disgrace may intervene to prevent an Alderman reaching the Chair, but on the whole most Aldermen in the fullness of time become first a Queen's Sheriff and, about four years later, Lord Mayor of London.

The Society of Apothecaries' Renaissance Hall, built in 1668 on a site which was originally the home of the Dominicans, or Black Friars. The entrance is in Blackfriars Lane and opens into a paved court. Walpole tells us that in 1784 the buildings on the eastern side of the court were built of brick and stone and adorned with columns of the Tuscan period, but in 1786 all the buildings surrounding the court were faced with stucco. Beneath the paving stones of the court there still exists the well from which the old friars obtained their water supply.

It was always a strictly male prerogative until November 1973 when Mrs Coven was elected for the aldermanic seat in the ward of Dowgate. She was rejected by the Court of Aldermen as not being 'a fit and proper person' to be admitted, on the grounds that she had misled the previous Lord Mayor about her intention to stand for election. At a second election for the ward two months later she was re-elected by fifty-three votes to twenty, but at a meeting of the Court of Aldermen her nomination was rejected once more. So far, therefore, her path to the Mansion House has been successfully blocked. How long the Aldermen can hope to do a Canute against the rising tide of

feminine ambition in the City is uncertain; what is quite beyond doubt is that they will defend to the last their very deep-rooted right to manage their own affairs.

The management of the City is based on a constitution which evolved in medieval times and has not changed much for over seven hundred years. William the Conquerer in fact never completely defeated the citizens of London, which is why the Tower was built outside the City boundaries. He compromised by granting them a separate charter and then in 1215 they won from King John the further concession of electing their own Mayor, whose power is still supreme within the square mile of the City. It says a great deal for the stability of this country that the system is still more or less unchanged. The Livery Companies are an important part of that stability. The Aldermen and Councilmen who make up the Corporation of the City are predominantly liverymen, although since the middle of the nineteenth century they do not have to be. In practice, however, there are no Aldermen and few Councilmen who do not belong to a Livery Company. This means therefore that not only do the livery elect the Lord Mayor and the Sheriffs, but it is from their ranks that the governing body of the City is drawn. Their fortunes like those of many great families have fluctuated with the swings of fate and the political pendulum, but they have managed to stand against the 'waves and weathers of time' to maintain their significance as an integral part of the system.

Architects model of the new Salters Hall, designed by Sir Basil Spence. It is being built in Fore Street to replace the one in St Swithin's destroyed by enemy action in 1941.

Jas. Record Sculp.

Sir William Wallworth

LORD MAYOR of LONDON

Chapter 1

History

It is a reverend thing to see an ancient building or castle not in decay; or to see a fair timber tree sound and perfect; how much more to behold an ancient noble family, which hath stood against the wages and weathers of time, for new nobility is but an act of power but ancient nobility is the act of Time.

SIR FRANCIS BACON

There are eighty-four Livery Companies flourishing root and branch in the City of London today, made up of the Great Twelve and seventy-two Minor Companies. For a proper understanding of their antiquity it is necessary to distinguish between a Company's first charter and the earliest date when it was known to exist. Since many guilds were operating several hundred years before they obtained a charter from the Crown, a Company's age can vary according to whether it is based on references in contemporary documents, or on the date of its first charter. Longevity sometimes depends on even more legendary material and the resulting confusion leaves scope for much benign rivalry as to which can lay claim to being the most ancient.

The Saddlers have a good case with an 1160 document, which refers to 'customs of old . . . when Sir Aernaldus was Alderman'. An Anglo-Saxon Master of the Company, who may even have been a contemporary of Alfred the Great, therefore gives them a thousand years of history to contemplate. Stow's *Survey of London* gives the Butchers a claim to existence in the tenth century: 'in the year 975 AD in the Ward of Farringdon, without the city walls, there are situated divers slaughter-houses and a Butchers' Hall where the craftsmen meet'. Some of the more legendary claims are based on the introduction of the craft itself, and go back as far as the Garden of Eden. In 1691 the poet Elkanah Settle, writing to please a Draper Lord Mayor, put forward a faultless case for the Drapers' early origins: 'Drapery is unquestionably so ancient as to have the honour of being the immediate successor of the fig leaves. And though we are not quite certain that our great first father began

An eighteenth-century engraving by James Record of Sir William Wallworth, Lord Mayor in 1381, who is shown holding the dagger with which he is supposed to have slain Wat Tyler.

it within his fair Eden, yet we are assured that Eve's spinstry and Adam's spade set to work together.' Anyone who dines with the Cutlers will probably know their claim, incorporated in the Company song:

> When Adam and Eve din'd on Apples and sal-lad,
> Keen hunger was Sauce to relish their Palate
> The man was contented and so was his Wife
> And they never once thought of the use of a knife.
> > Derry Down, Down, Down, Derry Down.

> But Eve soon grew tir'd of Diet so spare
> A Plum soon abhorr'd and detested a Pear
> Declar'd without Flesh, no joy was in life
> Of Flesh they had plenty, yet wanted a Knife.
> > Derry Down, etc.

> To please his fair Bride (tho' young in the Trade)
> Our Ancestor Adam a knife quickly made
> Tho' rough and unpolished yet all must agree
> He was the first Master of this Company.
> > Derry Down, etc.

The Founders Company do not stop even at the Garden of Eden. They imply direct descent from the deity Himself in their Company motto: 'God The Only Founder'.

References in old manuscripts, however, can depend upon prejudiced interpretation, records can perish and historians err; on the other hand the date of a charter is irrefutable. This is why no matter how many legendary claims may exist, a Company's official birth is taken from the date of its first charter, and by this criterion the Weavers, who obtained their Charter from Henry II in 1184, are the oldest.

The forerunners of the present Livery Companies originated in Anglo-Saxon times, and were concerned less with craftsmanship than with the salvation of souls. They were religious fraternities, grouped around a church, a monastery or a hospital, which the members used as a meeting place, and whose saint was adopted as patron. In times when death was a more present reality and hell-fire the inevitable fate of the damned, comfort in this life seemed less important than peace in the next. The fraternities were composed of simple men and women who spent much time praying for the souls of the departed and their first bequests were of monies to be spent on the celebration of masses for their souls. Funerals played an important part in the life of the communities, and even the poorest member was ensured a decent burial.

But the members of the fraternity might also be engaged in a common trade, since those who lived together often worked together; the bakers were all to be found in Bread Street, the basketmakers in Pudding Lane, or the drapers in Candlewick. It was therefore natural for them to combine the spiritual with the temporal and they developed into mutual protection societies, looking after the poor and needy in their communities and promoting the interest of their crafts. One of the early guilds which does not, however, seem to have had any religious background is the Fishmongers. Originating first by common usage, then by licence, there is no reference in early documents to religious or charitable motives; the sole aim seemed to be protection of the commercial interests of the members.

Although some guilds, such as the Weavers, the Bakers, and the Saddlers, sought official recognition from the start, common usage was a means by which many other guilds, including the Pepperers (later known as the Grocers), Goldsmiths, Fullers (known as Clothworkers), Butchers and Fishmongers, attempted to come into existence by themselves. However, alert Henry II was not a King to overlook such a fait accompli, and in 1179 he fined eleven 'adulterine guilds' for not seeking the royal assent.

The next hundred and fifty years brought favourable conditions in which the guilds were able to make steady progress, although times were hard and life uncertain. The Plantagenet rulers tended either to be warrior kings, often away campaigning for years on end, or else weak and easily led. The warriors made financial demands on the citizens with their military expenses and Richard Coeur de Lion, captured while returning from his third successful crusade, cost his loyal subjects

Detail from the Fishmongers' Funeral Pall, showing the arms of the Company, with mermaids on either side. This pall was embroidered by nuns about 1500, and was used for the lying in state of Fishmongers.

Merchant Taylors' crimson and gold funeral pall, dating from between 1490 and 1512. The side flaps consist of elaborately embroidered designs, illustrating the life and death of John the Baptist, patron saint of Merchant Taylors, sewn onto purple velvet, fringed with brown, yellow and green silk.

£100,000 in ransom money alone. The weaker Plantagenets, like King John, caused trouble of a different kind, through civil unrest brought about by intransigent barons and rioting mobs. However, a weak or absent ruler is an advantage to independently minded citizens trying to consolidate their position. By the end of the fourteenth century they had won many legal concessions, embodied in their charters, of which the power of search, the control of wages and prices and the licence in mortmain were the foundation on which they built their power.

The power of search gave each Company the right to inspect all goods handled by its members. The Wardens could seize or destroy any which in their opinion were sub-standard and punish the offenders. In medieval times when communications were difficult the areas of search tended to be limited to the City boundaries, although some of the charters contained powers for a wider jurisdiction. The Bakers Company, for instance, had control within the City and for a twelve-mile radius, the Pewterers the 'right of search within the City, the Suburbs and in any places throughout England'. At the height of their power this gave the guilds an effective weapon against competition from foreigners and a useful means of keeping their own members in line. Punishment befitted the crime and often involved a spell in the pillory, with the offending goods smouldering odorously below. For instance, in 1365 a Poulterer, John Russelle, was charged with exposing thirty-seven pigeons for sale, 'putrid, rotten, stinking and abominable to the human race, to the scandal, contempt and disgrace of the City'. He was sentenced to the pillory and the said pigeons were burnt under him. A notorious Pepperer who had sold various powders made of the 'root of rape and radish' in a putrified and unwholesome state, was made to stand in the pillory from eleven to twelve o'clock for three successive days, where his false powders were burned under his nose. The penalties for the baking of bad bread seem even more severe. For the first offence the unfortunate baker was drawn upon a hurdle from Guildhall to his own house with the faulty loaf hanging from his neck; for the second he suffered a similar disgraceful pilgrimage with the addition of an hour in the pillory, and, if he once again offended, his oven was pulled down and he was made to forswear the trade of baker in the City for ever. Short weight was equally vigorously dealt with, and the fear of infringing the law by mistake led to the introduction of the 'baker's dozen'. To avoid all risks of incurring a fine, master bakers used to give a surplus number of loaves called the 'inbread', and to make assurance doubly sure a thirteenth, which was called the 'vantage' loaf, was included with every twelve loaves.

There is no doubt that as well as making the guilds stronger these powers also did a great deal to maintain high standards of work among the London craftsmen. The Tylers and Bricklayers, who lost their powers of search in 1462 during the Wars of the Roses, claimed as an argument for the restitution of their rights, an instant deterioration in the workmanship of their craft. They argued that 'since inspection by the Fellowship had ceased tiles were so inefficiently wrought that instead of enduring for forty or fifty years, as they used to do, they lasted no more than three or four years'. This claim satisfied the Mayor, and the Tylers' right of search was restored to them. There was a case in 1708, by which time the Companies' control of their craft was weakened and searches less vigorously carried out, when the Tallow Chandlers Company were hoist with their own petard. A tallow chandler took the law against them and claimed damages for stock which the Company had destroyed in exercise of what it believed to be its rights. The Company lost the day, resulting in a heavy bill to foot, so wisely decided to abandon any further practice of its hereditary powers.

The control of wages and prices was another important weapon in the legal armoury of the guilds. Within a craft guild there were many strata. At the bottom were the apprentices, the lowest form of life during their seven years' servitude. Then there were the skilled journeymen, who were not allowed to work for anyone outside the Company without its permission. The livery were composed of those who could set up in business on their own, and it was from this body that the Master, Wardens and later in the fifteenth century, the Court of Assistants, were drawn. The running of the Company was therefore in the hands of the employers. They fixed the wages for the freemen and ensured that the apprentices were treated fairly and taught their trade. It was very difficult to trade in London unless you were a freeman of the City, and the only way to obtain such freedom was through membership of a guild, although under the 'custom of London' citizens free of one Company could practise the trade of any other.

In the early days the gap between Master and man was insignificant, and the apprentice could still hope to improve his fortunes overnight by marrying his Master's daughter, but as time went on and the guilds grew larger the differences between the livery and freemen increased. There was disrespect and dissatisfaction from the rank and file. The Armourers fined a member for calling the Court 'knaves and cheats' and his Master 'a rat-catcher's boy'. In the seventeenth century the Girdlers' artisans petitioned the King complaining that they had no more say in the running of the Company which, they said, had fallen into the hands of non-craftsmen. In other guilds the gap widened so far that the journeymen formed their own separate body called yeomen within the guild, and in the Ironmongers these yeomen even had their own separate Wardens. The old craft guilds cannot however be compared with the trade unions which developed later, since the guilds were always controlled and run by the master craftsmen and employers; their battles over demarcation and concern with wages and prices were in the interests of the employer and not of the worker.

The control of wages and prices was not only practised by the guilds themselves. The King often used the guilds to enforce price control. The first monarch to realize their potential in this respect was Edward III. When in 1362 a great tempest whipped the tiles off many a London roof, bringing good fortune to members of the Tylers Company, Edward intervened to prevent their capitalizing on the increased demand for their services by ordering that prices, and wages, which were 6d a day for the master and 4d for his men, 'should remain as hitherto and no higher rate be allowed'. Parliament met infrequently, but when it did many Members had to make the journey on horseback to London. In 1371, when he had called a meeting of Parliament, King Edward told the Innholders that the charge for feeding a horse for a day and a night was not to exceed 2½ d, the price for a gallon of best ale should be 2d, and a bushel of oats 6d. The chronicler does not stipulate whether the ale was for the horse or the thirsty politician.

Of all the powers the Ancient Guilds won from the monarchy the most important in the long term was the right to hold land and property in perpetuity. This licence in mortmain was the secret of their survival, for when their control of their craft weakened and their powers of search fell into desuetude, their strength remained in the freehold property which they possessed in the City of London. It may seem, looking back with the enchantment distance lends, that the bequests of houses or lands the old merchants made to their guilds were remarkably generous. However, such gifts were not entirely philanthropic. In a naughty world where an individual could look for no redress from the disasters brought about by Acts of God or man, the guild was the only permanency. Plague, fire or the sword fell on rich and poor alike; however powerful, no individual could escape the absolute authority of the monarch or the acquisitive grasp of a favoured minister; execution or imprisonment with ruin for his dependents threatened even the most wary. Only a corporate body such as a Livery Company had sufficient resources to weather such storms. A merchant would leave his house, some money or some land to his Company, so that his wife and children would benefit should he fall upon evil times. It was a medieval form of insurance, which was to yield far greater bonuses six hundred years later than the original donors could ever have foreseen.

In early days the guilds were concerned with providing the basic necessities of life, and so a look at the domestic histories of the individual Companies sheds an interesting light on what life was like for the ordinary Londoner. London in the fourteenth century was a walled city covering 677 acres. The fifty to sixty thousand men, women and children living within its walls were engaged in a great variety of occupations. It was a manufacturing town as well as the chief port of northern Europe. Bankers, shipowners and merchants lived side by side with craftsmen and victuallers.

The houses were made of timber and many were thatched with straw–a constant fire hazard. The streets were narrow and dirty, befouled by refuse thrown from the overhanging houses, and by horses and mules, which were the only form of transport. In 1400 the Pouche-makers Guild started to experiment with the making of the galoche, which was a sort of clog secured to the foot by a leather strap. There was no sign yet of the Pattenmakers, who developed the idea into effective protective

footgear in the sixteenth century, and so it is probable that
before 1400 the poor pedestrians were still plodding through
the mire of the London streets in their sandals.

The river was a more salubrious alternative for the wary pedestrian, and for any journey outside the city boundaries was
quicker, safer and cleaner. Consequently the Thames was
crowded with craft of every sort. By 1598 forty thousand men
earned their living on or about it. In cold winters it froze over so
completely that fairs and markets were held on the ice. The
romantic picture of Merrie England this evokes is somewhat
spoilt by referring to the Watermen's Company. Their members suffered sadly from loss of livelihood when the Thames was
frozen – so much so that provisions eventually had to be made
in their 1626 ordinances to pay a pension of 8d a week to be
granted to 'poor and impotent freemen of the Company'.

'London in Flames'—a contemporary engraving of the Great Fire of London 1666, published in Nuremberg by Christoper Lochner.

The fourteenth-century citizen was daily assailed by the sight, the sound and the smell of his 'daily bread'. Meat for his table came on the hoof to London and was sold live in the market-place to the butchers, who slaughtered the animals on the spot. There were two main market places for London: one at East Cheap, the other in Newgate Street, known more evocatively as St Nicholas' Shambles. The great market days were Mondays and Fridays, when the early mornings would be rent with lowing, bleating and the curses of the drovers, as with flaring torches to distinguish the owners' marks, they drafted into pens as many as 5,000 cattle and 26,000 sheep for sale at first light. Some of the work of the butchers was unpleasant for the passers-by, as instanced by a Royal Order in 1369, which called upon the Corporation to prevent the butchers from slaughtering their animals at St Nicholas' Shambles, carrying the offal through the lanes and streets to the jetty called Butchers' Bridge, and throwing it into the river.

Noise was a constant irritant. The clangour of iron being hammered into shape late into the night by armourers, blacksmiths, farriers and ironmongers disturbed the citizens and typical of their complaint is this description from Stow of how Lothbury came by its name:

> This street is possessed for the most part by Founders that cast candlesticks, chafing dishes, spice, mortars and such like copper or laton works and do afterwards turn them with the foot and not with the wheel, to make them smooth and bright with turning and scrating (as some do term it), making loathsome noise to the bypassers that have not been used to the like and therefore by them disdainfully called Lothberie.

But all was not dirt and disorder. London was a residential city too, with the houses of the nobility, the quiet and spacious monasteries and the homes of the wealthy merchants all adjacent to the busy, crowded streets. They were of course protected from the populace by their beautiful gardens, where flowers, fruit and vegetables for the household were grown. The first gardeners, however, seem to have had little support from their employers. When in 1345 they petitioned the Mayor to allow them to sell the garden produce of their masters, they were rejected on the grounds that 'their scurrility and clamour would disturb the priests at their prayers'.

Food preservation was a culinary science dependent upon salt or spice. The Salters, one of the Great Twelve Companies, rose to prominence and great wealth by reason of the demand for salt to cure fish and meat for winter provisions. Spices were in the hands of the Pepperers, founded in 1345, who later became known as the Grocers. They were armed with special powers for garbling, which meant cleansing or purifying spices, drugs and kindred commodities, and which gave them access to warehouses and shops anywhere in London. They also had charge of the King's Beam, which was the scale by which all heavy goods were weighed in the Port of London.

The medieval housewife had no problems with stubborn wrappings on her food, as the only form of packaging in existence then was a barrel or a basket. Since nearly every other Company depended upon their products for transporting their goods, it could be expected that the Coopers and the Basket-makers would be among the great and wealthy Companies of that period. However, this was not so. The Coopers Company, though undoubtedly old, never attained the rank and eminence of some of the others. They claim that in recognition of the important service they renderd to other crafts so long ago, they are now one of the first Companies the Lord Mayor visits after

Engraving of a Lord Mayor and Aldermen as they looked in Elizabethan times, from a manuscript in the British Museum.

LORD MAYOR AND ALDERMEN

Temp. ELIZABETH

MS. British Museum Add. 28330

his election. Basketmaking, one of the oldest of the primitive crafts, was practised at a very early date in London. However, the humble position of the craft amongst many wealthier communities prevented the formation of any efficient trade organization. It was established by an order of the Mayor's Court in 1569, but previously basketmaking seems to have been in the hands of those not free of the City, as they are mentioned a hundred years earlier in company with the Gold and Silver Wyre Drawers and 'other foreigners'.

Many materials in common use today were a luxury then which only the rich could afford. Glass was so dear and so scarce that until Henry VIII's reign it was as valuable as gold or silver. Glass windows were movables in fact and law. They were fitted into casements so that they could be stored away in safety when not in use. In law they were regarded as part of a man's personal possessions and not as part of his house. Those unable to afford such luxuries made do with horn. Even in the seventeenth century when glass became cheaper and more common, horn was considered more suitable for street lanterns, being a more robust material to withstand the rough and tumble.

In an age when violence was the only solution to many problems, street battles were spontaneous and common occurrences. The young apprentices were always getting into trouble fighting with rival crafts; often the quarrel escalated into something more serious and people got killed. To begin with the battles were against the 'foreigner', who might be a skilled worker coming to seek his fortune from abroad, or from outside the City. Then as more crafts came into existence the rivalries broke out among themselves. Too many guilds meant an overlapping of organizations. Four or five crafts would be involved in the production of one item. A suit of armour for instance was the work of the Armourers, Braisiers, Fourbers and Heumers. A simple thing like a knife was the work of many hands: the blade was made by the Bladesmiths, the handle by the Hafters, the sheath by the Sheathers and the Cutler was the man who assembled these diverse parts to complete the weapon. Even the Grinders and Furbishers could be in on the act. Naturally, demarcation disputes broke out. Everybody claimed the right of search of the finished product and blamed the others for shoddy workmanship. A quarrel between the Saddlers, Painters Stainers, Joiners and Lorimers ended in a bloody battle on Ascension Day in 1327, with many killed and injured. Order was restored by the intervention of the Mayor and the culprits were summoned to Guildhall. It took weeks to unravel the tangle of accusation, but the verdict eventually reached was that 'if the Saddlers ever again offended against the Joiners, Lorimers and Painters, they should be bound to pay ten tuns of good wine unto the Jointers, Lorimers and Painters within one month of the offence and in addition other ten tuns of good wine to the Mayor and Commonalty of London'. The same condition to apply to any Painter, Joiner or Lorimer who should offend against a Saddler.

By 1423 there were 111 craft guilds, which were obviously too many. Economic pressures brought about some rationalization. The Armourers absorbed all their competitors in a gradual process of consolidation: the Fourbers (furbishers and repairers) in 1367, the Heumers (helmet makers) in 1390, and Bladesmiths in 1515 and finally the Brasiers in 1708. At one time the Pursers, Glovers, Pouche-makers and Leathersellers were all in hot competition with each other. In 1498 the Pursers and Glovers merged in an attempt to solve their financial difficulties, but were eventually swallowed up by the Leathersellers, who also took over the Pouche-makers later, thus gaining a monopoly in the leather trade.

Civic strife was not always limited to street brawls and domestic quarrels among the crafts. The Masters and Wardens of some of the bigger guilds were rich and powerful merchants with political ambitions and a taste for intrigue. It was inevitable therefore that they should become involved in the battles of the Court. In Richard II's reign the guilds became embroiled in a long-drawn-out quarrel of great complexity, which eventually brought disaster on practically all the participants. The immediate bone of contention was food prices, which had the victualling guilds ranged against the mercantile guilds. The real quarrel was a symptom of the general malaise of the kingdom, exacerbated by the enmity between the King and his uncle John of Gaunt. On the King's side were the victuallers, activated by Nicholas Brembre, wealthy Grocer and Lord Mayor on several occasions. The mercantile trades were in Gaunt's party and they were led by John Northampton, an austere, reforming and very powerful Draper, also Lord Mayor on more than one occasion.

The first round went to the victuallers. When Wycliff came to St Paul's Cathedral to answer his accusers a great scuffle broke out in the name of religion, but which in reality was more concerned with the price of fish. The mob chased Gaunt to his Manor of Savoy and he was forced to slip away during the night before they sacked his home. Nicholas Brembre became Lord Mayor and for four years the victuallers had the upper hand.

However, by the time Wat Tyler was stirring up rebellion among the peasants, the power of the victuallers in the City was on the wane. They hoped to regain some of their lost popularity and aim a blow at Gaunt and his party by encouraging the Peasants' Revolt. So they opened the City gates to Wat Tyler and his band of rebels when they marched on London. By the time the mob had reached Smithfield, William Wallworth, then the leader of the Fishmongers Company, began to regret their part in the business. He drew his dagger, now a prized exhibit at Fishmongers Hall, and slew Tyler. With the death of their leader the rebellion quickly fizzled out.

It was now the turn of the mercantile trades to gain power. John Northampton became Lord Mayor and set about with reforming zeal to break the victuallers' monopoly of food prices. But reformers often lose favour with the fickle populace and soon the pendulum was once more swinging towards the victuallers. When Northampton saw power slipping from his grasp, he overplayed his hand in an attempt to halt the slide and ended up in Tintagel Castle on a charge of treason. He was lucky to escape with his life after two years' imprisonment and was banished from the City for good.

His downfall brought back the ambitious Grocer to the Mayoralty. Trusting in the King's support, Brembre cast aside all democratic pretence, used force to ensure his re-election at the Guildhall and terrified the citizens. But the prop on which he depended was an insubstantial support. King Richard II was too often the pawn of other more powerful players and in 1388 Parliament impeached the King's friends as traitors. Poor Brembre was tried and hanged for treason.

The seeds of religious reform that Wycliff was sowing at the time of this quarrel bore fruit a hundred years later in Henry VIII's reign. Although Henry used the pretext of religious reform for his own political and personal ends, the theological changes were very important to the religious institutions of the country. When Henry VIII came to the throne in 1509 the guilds were at the height of their power. In the days of their infancy as religious fraternities they had been protected by the Church's umbrella, but as they grew into powerful trade organizations with the economic life of the City in their hands, they were able to dispense with the Church's protection. Nevertheless they still had to pick their way warily through the doctrinal somersaults of the ensuing century. The materialistic reforms of Henry VIII, who dissolved monasteries and abbeys, but saved his soul for Rome, the fervid Protestantism of Edward VI and his advisers, the equally fervid Catholicism of Bloody Mary and Elizabeth's lukewarm compromise, all presented the guilds with a difficult path to tread. With their roots so firmly imbedded in religious soil, they had some very incriminating Catholic traditions to forsake.

The first attack, typical of Henry's reforming zeal, was upon their coffers. He did not object to masses for the dead in principle, only to endowments for this purpose. With this excuse he confiscated the money the guilds held in bequest for religious observances and much of their beautiful plate. On Edward vi's succession a stricter brand of Protestantism was introduced by his advisers. The guilds began to make prudent arrangements to divest themselves of the Catholic overtones they had inherited. The Brothers and Sisters of the guilds became known as Masters and Wardens. They unobtrusively abandoned the masses and prayers for the dead. The Coopers, for instance, in April 1554 resolved (on the plea of economy) to have neither mass nor sermon on their election day and in addition changed their motto from 'Gaude Maria Virgo' to 'Love as Brethren'. The Drapers had a coat of arms granted them by Henry vi in 1439 which included 'a representation in gold of the Virgin being crowned by God the Father with three Imperial Crowns which form part of the shield', but they applied for a new coat of arms during the reign of Elizabeth i, avoiding all mention of the Blessed Virgin.

The real threat to the guilds, however, was not so much religious as financial. The Tudors were not the first rulers to discover that the Companies were a convenient source of revenue; they just demanded more than their predecessors. No monarch was so short-sighted as to kill the goose that laid the golden eggs. In the absence of any more organized system, the guilds were an ideal medium through which to tax the citizens of London. The Crown sold legal rights in return for a cash payment and every charter granted to a Livery Company produced a new set of taxpayers for the royal revenue. When money was needed for a banquet or a battle the Lord Mayor was sent for and told what the City's contribution would be; he was a most convenient tax collector.

But nothing the Livery Companies had had to pay for so far matched the demands that they were to meet in the century to come. From 1603–88 they were the milch cow of the Crown, squeezed of every penny they could raise to ease the chronic Stuart penury. This was the worst period of their history. The Ulster colonization, the Civil War and the Great Fire of London brought them to such a state of financial despair that had it not been for the determination of the individual liverymen to sacrifice their own needs to those of their Company they would have been ruined. Looking at the Companies' history overall, it is not so much surprising that they are so old as that they survived the seventeenth century.

The Companies' involvement with the troubled province of

Ulster was made at the insistent invitation of James I. When the Irish rebellion—which in the latter part of Elizabeth's reign had brought about the downfall of her favourite the Earl of Essex—was eventually quelled, the lands and estates of the rebels O'Neill and O'Donnell became the property of the English Crown. It was inhospitable territory, inhabited by wild and dissident Irish chiefs and tribesmen. James I felt that could the civilizing influence of the citizens of London, and their organized system of administration, but be imposed upon these unruly bogmen, the province might become a model satellite of England. He therefore invited the Corporation of the City of London to undertake the colonizing of the counties Armagh, Tyrone, Derry, Donegal, Fermanagh and Cavan, in the hope that the Livery Companies would be attracted by a form of speculation which would bring them extensive land and property in addition to easing the over-population of the City. The Companies did not place as much faith in their ability to subdue the truculent Irish as did their monarch, but James renewed his invitation in terms they could not afford to refuse and fifty-five Companies eventually agreed under royal pressure to take part in the scheme.

A total of 290,950 acres was divided out among the Twelve Great Companies for an initial outlay of £60,000 in 1613. Each of the Twelve was joined by some of the Minor Companies, except for the Grocers who went in on their own. The Skinners, for instance, were joined by the Stationers, Girdlers and Bakers and were allotted 49,000 acres in all, of which 24,000 were bog and moor. The project got off to an expensive start in that each contribution was soon more than doubled by increased costs. The Companies found themselves having to chase their initial investment by throwing good money after bad and few of them ever saw much of a return on their capital. The Skinners seem to have succeeded best in turning the speculation to good account, perhaps by reason of having had among their members many practical surveyors who visited the domain personally. The Mercers, in association with the Cooks, Broderers and Masons, managed to stay with the Irish problem longer than most, but sold their estates in 1909, before 'the troubles' started.

Certainly as a financial speculation it was disappointing. As an expedient to solve the ills of the Ulster population, it was probably disastrous. The City of London merchants knew little of the problems of Ireland, and in view of what it was costing them, wished themselves well rid of their investment. As absentee landlords they left the administration of the land to those on the spot, many of whom merely compounded the existing evils, doing little to alleviate the poverty of their tenants or improve the fertility of the land.

The Companies were not helped by the policy of Charles I when he succeeded his father. Thinking that the Ulster colonization might make a convenient source of revenue for the Royal Exchequer, he annulled the charter of 1615 which had given the lands to the guilds. The Long Parliament in 1641 rescinded his act, and the Irish estates were once again restored to their reluctant owners by letters patent under Cromwell. But such royal inconsistency had crippled the power of the proprietors at a strategic moment in the development of the project.

The Civil War brought demands for money from both sides. In 1640 the guilds refused Charles £200,000 but had to lend him £40,000. At the outbreak of hostilities they contributed £100,000 towards the cost of Cromwell's army; raised another £500,000 for the relief of Gloucester and, at one stage in the campaign, provided £10,000 per week for the upkeep of the Train Bands. By this time some of the Minor Companies were in dire financial straits and in order to meet their share of such costs had had to sell all their plate.

On the whole the Companies were on the side of Parliament, although many individuals, such as Sir Richard Gurney, Lord Mayor when the battle started, were ardent royalists. The guilds' preference for the Puritan cause was somewhat weakened by the high-handed treatment they received from such commanders as Lord Fairfax. This forceful peer instructed a certain Colonel Dean to proceed with his force to the City and there to seize all such sums of money as he should find in the public treasury at Goldsmiths, Haberdashers and Weavers Halls, 'that by the said moneys I may be enabled to pay quarters whilst we lie hereabouts'. This seems poor return for the large sums the City had voluntarily subscribed. Whatever relief they may have felt in Cromwell's victory was therefore short-lived when they found that life under the Protector was not much easier than it had been before. Depressed by the solemnity of life under the Puritans and overawed by the army, by 1660 the Livery Companies like the rest of the country began to look back on the bad old days of the monarchy with nostalgia.

When Cromwell died and General Monk went to France to invite Charles II to resume the throne, the guilds prepared to welcome him back as eagerly as the rest of his people. Generously they dipped into their dwindling resources to find the money to put on a show lavish enough to express their loyalty. The new King promised them future privileges and

immunities, new favours to advance their trade, wealth and honour. In a spirit of happy euphoria therefore they spent £6,000 on the procession to escort Charles II through the City streets from the Tower to Whitehall before his coronation. All too soon the honeymoon was over. Charles II turned out to be a bigger spender than any of his forebears. His determination to be free of the necessity of asking Parliament for money and his extravagant nature meant that he was always looking for new sources of revenue. But it was not from the King that the worst blow was to fall.

Around midnight on the first of September 1666 fire broke out in a baker's shop in Pudding Lane and, fanned by a strong easterly wind, it soon set light to the timber buildings of the City. For three days nothing could halt its terrible progress; 89 churches, 13,200 houses, 400 streets, the Guildhall, Livery Halls, libraries, schools and hospitals were totally destroyed. The ash, all that was left of these homes, covered an area of 436 acres. Samuel Pepys' eye-witness account in his diary describes the fire growing,

> and as it grew darker, appeared more and more, and in corners and upon steeples, and between churches and houses, as far as we could see up the hill of the City, in a horrid malicious bloody flame, not like the fine flame of an ordinary fire. We stayed till, it being darkish, we saw the fire as only one entire arch of fire from this to the other side of the bridge, and in a bow up the hill for an arch of above a mile long; it made me weep to see it. The churches, houses, and all on fire and flaming at once; and a horrid noise the flames made, and the crackling of houses at their ruin.

The Great Fire is considered by subsequent generations to have been a blessing in disguise, for it destroyed much that was ugly and insanitary, and is generally believed to have burnt out any infection lingering from the Great Plague the year before. However, for the Livery Companies it was an unmitigated disaster because it destroyed their property, one of the fundamental sources of their income. There was no insurance nor compensation to cushion the blow. In fact the richer Companies were hardest hit, since they had more to lose. Halls, almshouses and the accumulated inheritance of the past four hundred years had been reduced to dust within three days. The only resources they could call on for rebuilding were the sale of any plate saved from the fire and contributions from individual members.

At the end of Charles' reign an attempt was made by the King to curb the power of the City by giving the control of the Livery Companies to the nominees of the Crown. This he did by issuing a Writ of *Quo Warranto* by which the Companies had

The earliest surviving English Grant of Arms, which was made to the Drapers Company on 10th March 1439, by William Bruges, Garter King of Arms in the reign of Henry VI.

either to hand in their charters or prove their right to hold them. Debilitated by their financial losses, and with little hope of legal victory, the Companies surrendered to this additional psychological attack. On payment of a fine they were granted new charters, giving them the customary rights over their trade but with no choice in the election of their Masters and Wardens. Had Charles lived longer he might well have succeeded in gaining control of the Livery Companies and indirectly the City, but he died before his policy had had time to work. He was succeeded in 1685 by confusion and his brother James II. Although James was anxious to curry favour with the City, he does not seem to have improved matters very much and it was not until 1689 when William and Mary came to the throne that the guilds won a re-grant of all their powers and a period of peace in which to rebuild their shattered fortunes.

The past two hundred years, although disastrous for the Companies, had not arrested the work of the individual craftsmen. Progress was being made in trade and craft alike, which brought a degree of comfort to the seventeenth-century citizen unknown to his fourteenth-century counterpart and many guilds had become established to cater for more sophisticated tastes.

The ships of Drake and Raleigh exploring unknown waters in Elizabeth's reign brought back from their sorties plunder from Spanish galleons and new materials for the craftsmen to try out. They also brought tobacco. The habit the English seafaring men had picked up from the Spanish, French and Portuguese sailors was quickly emulated by the fashionable dandies around the Court. It did not find favour, however, with James I who, in his *Counterblast to Tobacco* in 1604, condemned the custom as 'loathsome to the eye, hateful to the nose, harmful to the braine, daungerous to the Lungs, and in the blacke stinking fume thereof, nearest resembling the horrible Stigian smoke of the pit that is bottomelesse'. But his prejudice against smoking did not conflict with his economic sense and James granted the Tobacco Pipe Makers a charter in 1619.

The Haberdashers found a commercial winner in the pin. £50,000 is said to have been paid annually to foreigners at first for this little item, but by the end of Elizabeth I's reign the Haberdashers were making it themselves. Pins were so essential and expensive a part of the well-dressed woman's wardrobe, that husbands allowed their wives an extra allowance which was called 'pin money', with which to purchase them.

Clocks, which had originally been made by freemen of the Blacksmiths Company, became a work of art in themselves.

Garden of Stationers Hall, where a plane tree now grows on the spot where heretical books, condemned by the ecclesiastical authorities, were once burned by the Wardens of the Company.

The Triumphall Entertainment of ye King and Queenes maties by ye Right honoble ye Lord Maior and Cittizens of London at their coming from Hampton-court to Whitehall (on ye River of Thames) Aug: ye 23 1662.

Agua

There were many craftsmen making complicated and beautiful time-pieces who were outside the Blacksmiths Company and they wanted a guild of their own. In 1631 they petitioned Charles I for a charter and founded the Association of the Master, Wardens and Fellowship of the Art or Mystery of Clockmaking of the City of London.

In 1628 the Makers of Playing Cards appeared. Until the beginning of the century most cards were imported from France, but by this time there were enough English card makers to give them the monopoly. The Charter of the Makers of Playing Cards therefore forbade the import of any foreign playing cards and the Company undertook to make up for the consequent loss in customs duty by a payment of two shillings per gross on all playing cards, and a further one shilling per gross for the receiving officer. The Glovemakers, who had been taken over by the Leathersellers in 1502, benefited now that gloves had become a costly and ornamental fashion accessory. The demand for gloves brought about such an expansion in their trade that they were able to form their own guild again.

The setting up of Caxton's printing press in 1476 made books

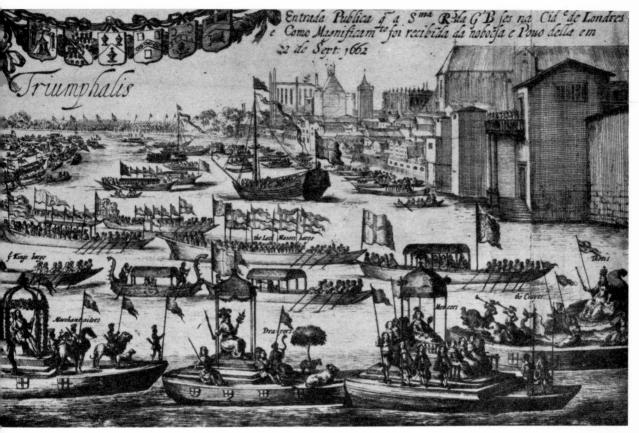

Entrada Publica q̃ a Sma Rʸa GᵃBˢ fes na Cidᵉ de Londres e Como Magnificamᵗᵉ foi recibida da nobeſſa e Pouo della em 22 de Sept: 1662

Triumphalis

more readily available for the few people outside the Church who could read, and eighty years later the demand for literature was such as to necessitate a guild to regulate the trade. The Stationers Company, who had previously dealt only in paper and material for book binding, received a charter giving them control of copyright. Maybe the increased literacy put a strain on the eyes of the populace, as the Spectacle Makers, who until 1629 were too small an industry to have a guild of their own, now became incorporated.

The first pair of silk stockings appeared in Elizabeth's reign. They were hand-knitted and presented by Mrs Montague to the Queen in the presence of the gallant Lord Leicester and statesmanlike Lord Burleigh. Leicester urged the Queen to try the new hose, which she had thought too frail to wear, saying 'My gracious Lady, they are fit for the fairies to wear and your gracious Majesty is all beautiful, in fact a fairy queen wanting but this gossamer wear to perfect fairy attire'. Burleigh was more prosaic in his advice, saying that he thought honest cloth was good enough for everyone to use and that her wearing of such things would upset the cloth hose trade. He overplayed the practical approach by suggesting that no human leg could

'Aqua Triumphalis' is one of a series of seven contemporary engravings by R. Stoop. It shows the triumphal entertainment of King Charles II, and his bride Catherine of Braganza, by the Lord Mayor and Citizens of London, at their coming from Hampton Court to Whitehall on the River Thames on 23rd August, 1662.

get into such fragile things. Elizabeth's vanity was immediately piqued and she retired to her private apartments for an hour with the new stockings. When she returned she was in one of her best moods and laughingly informed her two advisers: 'Gentlemen, the silk stockings fit me right well, and I like them much, because they are pleasant, fine and delicate, and henceforth I will wear no more cloth stockings.' The Queen's vanity resulted in eventual prosperity for the Framework Knitters, and in 1657 they received a charter of incorporation from Oliver Cromwell. The Needlemakers are the only other guild to have received a charter from the Protector.

The Restoration saw the coach, which had first appeared in Elizabeth's reign, become an accepted though cumbersome mode of travel. Much elaborate design and cunning craftsmanship went into its manufacture, bringing plenty of work for the coachbuilders, who in 1677 were incorporated into the Coachmakers and Harness Makers Guild. Ladies could now journey in a manner more suited to their fragility, though the roads they had to travel on were still little better than cart-tracks. The London streets were as muddy as ever, which meant plenty of business for the Pattenmakers.

In James I's reign the supply of medicine—rudimentary though it was compared to our pill-ridden age—began to be considered scientific enough to merit a special guild. The control of drugs was taken away from the Grocers and given to the Society of Apothecaries who were incorporated in 1617. The Grocers protested vehemently to James, whose ambiguous reply was that

> The mistery of these Apothecaries was belonging to the Apothecaries, wherein the Grocers are unskilful and therefore I think it fitting that they should be a Corporation of themselves. They [the Grocers] bring home rotten wares from the Indies, Persia, and Greece, and herewith thro' mixtures make water and sell such as belong to the Apothecaries.

If a malady was beyond the help of herbs or drugs then the sufferer had to put his faith in God and his body in the hands of the Barber-Surgeons. Blood letting had originally been performed by the clergy—perhaps as a desperate attempt at saving life before they administered the last rites. However, Pope Alexander felt it an unseemly occupation for priests and in 1163 put a stop to their participation. The task then fell to the Barbers, who by reason of their skill with the razor had assisted the clergy. In Henry VIII's reign the Barbers Company was amalgamated with the Surgeons by Act of Parliament. A surgeon's skill was only as good as his knowledge of the human

A line engraving for Harrison's 'History of London', 1776, which shows the sort of dress which was worn by a Lord Mayor and a Merchant around 1640.

body he was trying to cure and doctors were short of cadavers on which to practise their art. However, the Company was allowed four dead felons a year for dissection, an arrangement for which one William Duell had good cause to be thankful. In 1740 Duell was convicted of rape and murder and hanged at Tyburn and his body presented to the Barber-Surgeons. He was a little fellow weighing only about six stone and not heavy enough for hanging alone to kill him. Since his neck had not been broken by the rope the malefactor came back to life on the dissecting table. The Company dutifully sent him back to Newgate prison, but since it is impossible to be hanged twice for the same crime, Duell was deported to Australia, where it is believed he spent his life a reformed character and perpetually grateful to the Company of Barber-Surgeons.

The last of the guilds to appear at this period was the Fanmakers Company in 1709. The fan, which first appeared in England at the time of Elizabeth I, grew increasingly important as an accessory of the elegant woman of fashion, until in the eighteenth century it reached such significance in the language of formal flirtation that no drawing-room dalliance was complete without one.

By the time the Fanmakers had become established as a guild, many of the older Companies had already lost their trade connections. The Mercers were one of the first to do so, and 150 years earlier, when Queen Elizabeth had asked them why silk was so dear, they had only been able to reply that none of their members was engaged in the silk trade. Admission by patrimony meant that as time went on fewer members of a Company were engaged in its craft. This system of hereditary privilege, which brought non-craftsmen into the guilds, meant that when the trade element in the Company weakened they still had a membership of wealthy and influential men who played an important part in the life of the City and were in a position to contribute liberally to the Company's coffers.

But not all Companies were able to attract influential outsiders or acquire the rich sons of former tradesmen. Some guilds struggled along on their own, their prosperity depending upon the fluctuations of their craft. Those who still relied on their trade to make them viable suffered from the introduction of steam power in the eighteenth century and the great expansion in production that followed. The way in which a guild operated had been designed for a small, closely knit community and a guild's power rested in its monopoly over its trade. Once demand outstripped the ability of the members of the guild to satisfy it, the battle against the 'foreigner' was lost. The growing prosperity in the reigns of Queen Anne and the Georges brought so much work that it became possible to prosper in London without being a freeman of the City. Once the majority of craftsmen could earn their living successfully without having to belong to a guild, or to subject themselves to its restrictive ordinances, the guilds lost their control.

The Livery Companies now had to find a new role. For those with influence and status it was easy. They continued to attract rich and generous benefactors and they also possessed land and property, which was increasing in value in step with the growing importance of the City. The little plots of land they had inherited from the medieval merchants had now become valuable freehold. All they had to do was to watch it grow, administer their charities and entertain their members. For the poorer Companies it was not so easy. Those who had no livery status could not even offer political rights, which until 1832 included the privilege of being able to vote for Members of Parliament for the City. The Company cupboard was bare after the tribulations of the seventeenth century and now they had lost the means of replenishment. While the big Companies grew fat and complacent, the little ones were in danger of dying a natural death. The Carmen were reduced to three members, the Horners to 15, the Needlemakers were dying and the Gardeners and Paviours were extinguished for a time.

What rejuvenated them all was the radicalism of the late nineteenth century. To the poorer Companies it brought an infusion of new blood, and to the richer the threat of persecution which put them on their mettle. Tory politicians, frightened that the growing tide of liberalism might sweep away many fine English institutions, including themselves, thought that the Livery Companies might help to stem the flood. They encouraged committed Tories to take part in City politics by buying their freedom in the City Companies. At last some of the dying Companies had something to offer new members. They applied to the Court of Aldermen to increase the numbers they were permitted on their livery and those who were still only guilds applied for livery status.

The Liberals were aware of what was going on and accused various Companies of attempting to resuscitate their guilds on political grounds. The Needlemakers when so accused explained that they had heard that a number of gentlemen were desirous of joining a City Guild and who, hearing of the Needlemakers, decided to offer themselves as candidates. The livery was therefore enlarged under the sanction of the Court of Aldermen to accommodate them.

Mr Gladstone's attack in 1884 was a more determined attempt to pull the rug from under the Tories. It took the form of a Royal Commission of Enquiry into the activities of the Companies. Like most Royal Commissions it was something of a blunt instrument since no action was taken on its findings. The opinion of the investigators seems to have been a little divided as to the usefulness of the continued existence of the guilds. However, the majority felt that the Companies had satisfactorily proved that they were administering the funds they had inherited, not only for the charitable purposes for which they were intended, but also 'for others directly or indirectly connected with education, social science and human progress'. The Ancient Guilds had been vindicated.

They had also been jolted out of their complacency. Always at their best when under attack, they now began to bestir themselves to take a greater interest in their trade. They realized that it was not enough to indulge in vague medieval philanthropy and secret benevolence. They must more openly be seen to be doing good.

The resulting activity put them more in touch with contemporary life and certainly by the beginning of this century they were more commercially awake. So much so that when the Master Mariners were thinking of getting together in some sort of trade organization in the 1920s, the idea of a Livery Company did not seem too far fetched. They restricted their membership to those holding a Master's certificate, and were granted a charter by George v in 1929, together with the privilege of calling themselves the Honourable Company of Master Mariners. Others followed their lead and six new Companies have been granted liveries since the Second World War: the Solicitors, the Farmers, the Air Pilots and Air Navigators, the Tobacco Pipe Makers and Tobacco Blenders (a revival of the old Company), the Furniture Makers and the Scientific Instrument Makers.

So the position of the guilds and Livery Companies today appears to be a very secure one. Persecution from premiers or the Crown seems a thing of the past. Their relations today with the monarchy have never been better and seventeen Companies now have members of the Royal Family as liverymen, freemen or honorary freemen. It was in the Guildhall that the Queen and the Duke of Edinburgh publicly celebrated their twenty-fifth wedding anniversary in November 1972, a token of the continued close connection between the City and the sovereign. The Companies continue to administer charitable and educational funds unmolested, supporting their trades with encouragement for high standards of design and workmanship, and there is no shortage of men and women wishing to join their ranks.

Yet there has been no room for complacency, for the last hundred years have brought disaster and also a great need for adaptability. The damage to Livery Company properties during the Second World War bombing was as extensive as their losses in the Great Fire in the seventeenth century, but the task of rebuilding their ancient halls in a modern city was an aesthetic as well as a financial challenge. The rate of social and technological progress over the last hundred years has been spectacular in comparison with that in the centuries before. The welfare state has taken over much of their charitable work and scientific invention has made many a Company's interests archaic. The biggest problem they are dealing with now therefore is that of fitting their five-hundred-year-old institutions into the twentieth century in such a way as to preserve their interesting heritage without becoming totally anachronistic.

Chapter 2

Halls

Now I remember
We met at Merchant Taylors' Hall at dinner
In Threadneedle Street.
            Sir Moth, in *The Magnetic Lady* by Ben Jonson, 1632

Is a hall really necessary, one might ask? The Companies who have gone to such trouble and expense to rebuild since the war would answer in the affirmative, but the fact is that over half the guilds now manage without one. Some, like the Gold and Silver Wyre Drawers, the Clockmakers, or the Feltmakers, were never rich enough to afford the luxury of their own hall; others, like the Weavers, were unable to maintain their halls when their fortunes declined; many unfortunates, like the Cordwainers, the Coachmakers, the Coopers, the Joiners and Ceilers and the Parish Clerks, lost their halls in the blitz and were unable to face the enormous cost of rebuilding.

The use to which a hall is put varies enormously from Company to Company, as does the accommodation it contains. Basically a livery hall is used for transacting the business of the Company and for the entertainment of its members. All halls contain at least a banqueting or livery hall and a court room. Most of them also have drawing rooms, court dining rooms, parlours, libraries and even a flat for the Master; Companies still involved in aspects of their trade also have the administrative offices necessary to carry out this function. Like many stately homes, the halls are now open for public viewing several times a year and visits are arranged by the Information Centre beside St Paul's Cathedral.

The Merchant Taylors and the Goldsmiths were the only crafts known positively to have possessed halls before 1400 and at first the members of a guild met in monastic houses, taverns or the homes of their more affluent members. Then they either purchased or were bequeathed a suitable house for the Company's headquarters and by 1500 twenty-eight guilds had halls of their own. By then the possession of a hall was a sign that a Company had arrived. The first halls were comprehensive dwellings, with gardens, Clerks' houses, armouries and granaries as well as a banqueting hall for the livery and offices for conducting the Company's affairs.

The Plaisterers Hall of 1669 contained the following:
One kitchen under the Great Hall, One Buttery – Two little Cellars – a Coal hole and one great Cellar under the Parlour and the Room going into the Garden – one little Parlour under the Lobby and one great Parlour even with the said little Parlour – One large Room or Chamber with a Closet lying over the said great Parlour – and one little Room or Chamber lying even with the said Great Room or Chamber and little Room aforesaid and the Common Hall.

By reason of their size and ability to accommodate large meetings, the halls were used by bodies other than guilds, who lacked suitable meeting places of their own. Many well-known institutions were founded or held their first meetings in, for instance, the Mercers Hall, including the East India Company, the Bank of England, the Board of Trade, the Royal Exchange Assurance (originally named 'The Mercers Hall Marine Company') and, more recently, the City and Guilds of London Institute. Nowadays the halls are sought after more for the special ambience they can give to a party, but the Companies are very selective in their choice of those they allow in. Opinion varies as to the suitability of using the hall itself for gain. Some Companies lend but never hire, others pass on a proportion of their expenses for lighting, heating etc. but make no profit, others regard hiring out their hall as a legitimate means of offsetting the cost of owning it. A Company like the Goldsmiths maintains an attitude of noblesse oblige in the use of its hall, lending it for concerts, jewellery exhibitions, lectures and many charitable functions or trade occasions. The day-to-day running of the Company is as complex as many big commercial enterprises and so the hall is something of a cross between the head office of a City bank and a stately home.

The halls with the best ambience are the ones with a good period atmosphere. Unfortunately few halls are architecturally coherent, having been ravaged by death watch beetle and the improving zeal of succeeding generations. But by far the worst damage has been by fire. Livery halls were always burning down, embellished as they were with so much fine timber panelling. As recently as 22 September 1965 the Grocers Hall caught fire and within a few hours was almost completely destroyed. The blaze spread so quickly that only the Records and silver could be saved. In 1666 forty-four out of the existing

fifty-one halls were destroyed by the Great Fire. Samuel Pepys conveys the helplessness of the citizens when he describes meeting the Lord Mayor, 'exhausted with a handkerchief round his neck crying: "Lord! What can I do? I am spent: people will not obey me. I have been pulling down houses but the fire overtakes us faster than we can do it".' In the Second World War sixteen halls were totally destroyed and fourteen badly damaged; on two occasions, once in 1940 and again in 1941, it seemed as if the whole of London was burning. The bombing interfered with the supply of water and those trying to save the buildings were as helpless as the seventeenth-century fire-fighters had been. There was no Pepys in an air-raid warden's helmet scribbling for posterity, but plenty of people still remember the feeling of impotence as they watched the flames fiercely consuming London's historical heritage.

A contemporary account from the records of the Cutlers Company paints a vivid picture of the scene on an evening in December 1940:

> There was a fresh, light wind to fan the flames and for some reason the water pressure failed so that no hoses could be used and the firemen stood by powerless. For two hours the great fire raged, eating up building after building in its greedy fury and every minute creeping nearer to our Hall . . . two great fires bearing down—one raging up Warwick Lane and the other along Newgate Street.

The account goes on to say that when all seemed lost the Beadle, with his wife, was ordered to leave, but he refused to quit his post and took up his stand on the steps of the GPO building in Newgate Street 'to see what was going to happen to the old Hall' and 'to keep an eye on the wine cellar'. It seemed as if nothing could save the hall from the fate suffered by the rest of Warwick Lane, when suddenly the waiting firemen heard the welcome sound of water in the hoses: the pressure built up, and the hungry flames were checked and slowly beaten back.

Armourers Hall owes its survival to the action of an unknown fireman that same Sunday evening. Seeing the curtains of the court dining room ablaze he broke in and extinguished the

Terracotta frieze from the front of Cutlers Hall, illustrating the various processes of the cutler's art. It was the work of a young cutler called Creswick, who had a considerable reputation for monumental tombstone statuary. The faces of the figures on the frieze are said to be those of Creswick's fellow-workers in Sheffield, and it is believed to be the only existing accurate representation of the trade of cutlery as exercised in Victorian times.

flames. His identity could never be established, but he undoubtedly saved the hall.

Of the halls not totally destroyed, seven still retain some renaissance origins, of which the Apothecaries is the finest period piece. It is situated in a quiet courtyard behind Blackfriars Station on a site which was originally the home of the Dominicans, or Black Friars, who came to England in 1221. The present hall was built by the Apothecaries in 1668 after the Great Fire. It had a lucky escape this century when during the war a bomb fell through the roof and down three floors to the basement of an adjoining building without exploding. Although the entrance hall looks contemporary with the rest, it was in fact reconstructed in 1929. However, the lovely original staircase of 1671 with its fine carving more than makes up for any discrepancy of dates and the atmosphere is at least four hundred years old. From the walls of the banqueting hall pictures of past Masters look solemnly down, their expressions as sombre as the aged timbers of the 1671 panelling. Displayed in the parlour is a now valuable collection of apothecaries' jars and porcelain pill slabs, the latter being the forerunners of the modern diplomas. Before the introduction of paper certificates, the qualified dispenser used to hang his pill slab up upon his wall, which was proof of his licence to practise.

Another hall which retains much of its original seventeenth-century character is the Stationers, tucked away in its own serene courtyard, behind the new shopping precincts to the north of St Paul's Cathedral. The Stationers, like the Apothecaries, benefited architecturally from not being an affluent Company in the nineteenth century, when many of the richer ones pulled down their attractive renaissance halls to make way for something grander. The Stationers Hall was given a new façade in 1800 and although considerably damaged in the war, restoration work was carried out carefully to simulate the design of the old building. In the ancient courtyard a leafy plane tree flourishes, where once heretical books which had been condemned by the Church authorities were burnt by members of the Company.

Half-way down Dowgate Hill elaborate wrought-iron gates bar entry to a tiny inner courtyard almost completely occupied by a Catalpa – an Indian bean nut tree. This is the forecourt to the Tallow Chandlers Hall, who have occupied the site since they bought it for £166 13s. 4d. in 1476. Their charming little hall was built in 1672 and much of the oak panelling is original. The ceiling in the banqueting hall dates from 1868 and round the walls hang the arms of the twenty other Companies which the Tallow Chandlers allow to use the hall. Some beautiful painted leather screens on the staircase are seventeenth-century and the overall impression is that of an attractive house which has grown old gracefully.

Nearby in College Street is one of the smallest, the Innholders Hall. Looking exactly like the perfect place to stop for a change of horses or the night, it could be a model for a nineteenth-century inn. Although rebuilt in 1885 it still retains a 1670 ceiling, wall panelling and chimney pieces. The only public rooms are a cosy anteroom and the banqueting hall, but it has a first-class atmosphere for a small party.

Round the corner is the Skinners Hall, which is of course much grander. The continued prosperity of the Company in the eighteenth and nineteenth centuries meant that the hall acquired many later additions to its seventeenth-century structure. The beautiful old staircase dates from 1670, as does much of the panelling. The court room, panelled in Virginian pencil cedar, is famous for its pungent aroma, which did not escape the notice of Macaulay. In his *History of England* he records that the Company met 'in a parlour renowned for the fragrance which exhaled from a magnificent wainscot of cedar'. The ceiling of the entrance hall, which was badly damaged in the war, has been raised, improving the proportions of the room. It is now the perfect place to hang the magnificent glass chandelier, which was made in Russia in one of the glass factories sponsored by Potemkin and brought to England in about 1784. The banqueting hall has a nineteenth-century sombre splendour that is particularly suitable to the formal dining habits of Livery Companies. High on the walls a set of twelve mural paintings by Sir Frank Brangwyn adds richness to the dark panelling below, making the Skinners' banqueting hall one of the most impressive in the City.

Though wrapped in an outer coating of Victoriana, the Vintners Hall contains some rare relics of its renaissance origins, including the oldest inhabited room in the City. The elaborately decorated panelling of their court room was completed after nine years' work in 1676 and is original. Elsewhere the panelling has been more susceptible to the effects of death watch beetle and central heating, and is constantly having to be renovated, renewed or treated. The old staircase is enriched by much elaborate carving typical of Charles II's reign, especially the newel posts. Of the carving elsewhere the Company is proudest of the wooden sword rest hanging in the banqueting hall. It is unusual to find one in the City made of wood. The Vintners' is carved with vine ornament in the centre part and grapes decorating the sides. The ceiling of the hall, which is a Wren copy hung in the 1930s, is also decorated with vines, bunches of grapes and other flora and fauna associated with wine making. It has recently been painted in bright blues and purples, which contrasts startlingly with the dark panelling of the walls.

Although the Merchant Taylors Hall has twice been completely gutted by fire, once in 1666 and again in 1940, on both occasions the walls and foundations survived, and so it still has parts that are older than any of the other halls. Outside it is a mixture of the baronial Gothic of the 1870s, some original seventeenth-century brickwork with here and there a medieval stone or two. The paved courtyard round which the hall is built has been there since 1347. The old kitchen in the basement survived both fires and has been in continuous use since 1425; its great stone walls and lofty ceiling were designed for a time when the preparation of feasts needed more room for manoeuvre, but now a smaller modern kitchen has been built within the old framework. A large and blackened spit stands idle in one corner, a reminder of the more primitive culinary methods of the past. The interior of the hall is a modern work of reconstruction. The large banqueting hall is panelled in mahogany, the stained glass windows decorated with the arms of honorary freemen. At the far end of the hall above the wide gallery is a very fine Renatus Harris organ. This instrument was built originally for the Church of St Dionis Backchurch in Fenchurch Street in 1722 and was the last organ Harris built. It was allowed to fall into disrepair on several occasions and was moved around from church to church and from institution to institution. Eventually it was removed from Dartford by the Merchant Taylors in 1962 and restored once again to full decorative and musical order. As much as possible of the original Harris pipework has been retained and Merchant Taylors Hall is now in great demand for all kinds of musical evenings. The Company seem to have had great success recently in finding period works of art with which to decorate the modern interior of their hall. One of the drawing rooms is papered with very pretty eighteenth-century Chinese hand-painted wallpaper which the then Clerk of the Company recently discovered in an auction room and bought for the Company.

It is sad that there should be only one genuine Georgian hall left: this is the little hall of the Watermen and Lightermen's Company, designed by William Blackburn in 1780. There are only two main rooms, a parlour, and a court room with a lovely painted ceiling in the rose, green and blue pastel colours of the Georgian period. Since they can only seat thirty-seven in this room, for annual livery dinners the Company borrows the Fishmongers Hall.

The Fishmongers have inhabited their site on the banks of the Thames since 1434, and this is the third hall to be built there. It is one of the seven Victorian livery halls left and was built by the Company in 1834 when the seventeenth-century hall had to be pulled down to make way for the new London Bridge. Although it has plenty of the marble and ornate decoration typical of grand buildings in the nineteenth century, it has far less of the dark panelling so common in other livery halls. Designed by Henry Roberts it is now generally recognized to be one of the finest examples of the Greek Revival style. Roberts planned the building so that all the principal rooms were on the first floor, to take advantage of the magnificent river site, and the overall effect is a light and airy grandeur. The motif of a dolphin, symbol of the Fishmongers Company, is used extensively in decoration. Entwined around pillars, creeping up legs, propping up the arms of chairs, or inset into marble floors, these friendly sea creatures are everywhere. The Company has many ancient treasures on display, relics from its past and expensive

Merchant Taylors Hall in Threadneedle Street. The first Hall was built here between 1347 and 1392, and does not appear to have been substantially altered until the roof and interior were gutted in 1666 in the Great Fire of London. The Great Kitchen survived and is still in use today, having also survived when the Hall was again gutted by fire from incendiary bombs in September 1940. Certain parts of the premises escaped damage, however, including the Library with its collection of early books, first editions and other old volumes principally dealing with London.

acquisitions, which testify to a long and prosperous history. But it is not only treasures of the past for which the Fishmongers are famous. Annigoni's portrait of the Queen, which the Company commissioned and which now hangs in the court drawing room, has given it a reputation for perspicacity in the encouragement of modern artists too.

The two grandest nineteenth-century halls still left are the Goldsmiths and the Drapers. Whatever can be said about the aesthetic value of the Victorians' architecture, there is no doubt that they were very good at creating an atmosphere of formal opulence. Solid marble columns and alabaster staircases, stained glass windows and portraits of British sovereigns, Florentine ceilings painted in 1900, crystal chandeliers and massive marble fireplaces speak eloquently of wealth and importance. Amid the impressive opulence of the Drapers Hall there are also some touches of antiquity, an eighteenth-century ceiling in the court room, a seventeenth-century one in the court dining room, and a superb eleven-foot-high walnut grandfather clock in the vestibule. The mulberry trees in the garden are remarkable for their longevity – one of them dates back to the time of James I – and their fecundity, since they still bear fruit each year to make delectable mulberry pies for the first court luncheon in the autumn.

The Goldsmiths Hall is imposing rather than opulent, as befits a Company still so involved in the activities of its trade. The hall personifies the might of nineteenth-century England, and is summed up by a contemporary description at its opening in July 1835 as being 'marked by an air of palatial grandeur not exceeded by that of any other piece of interior architecture in the metropolis'. Behind the Prime Warden's chair in the court room is a Roman stone altar to Diana from the second century, which was found in 1830 during excavations for the foundations for the new hall.

Anyone accidentally straying into the Armourers Hall would not long remain in doubt as to which Company it belonged, since everywhere are relics of the Armourers' trade. The medieval weaponry does not seem out of place among the nineteenth-century surroundings and the banqueting hall is the most dramatic of any in the City in which to dine: the panelled walls are decorated with the coats of arms of past Masters; overhead hang solid brass chandeliers purchased by the Company in the middle of the eighteenth century; high up under the roof the stained glass window with its red cross of St George is floodlit from outside; and on the walls spears, helmets, breastplates, swords and pikes glisten in the flickering candlelight.

The Cutlers Hall in Warwick Lane is more like a Victorian country house than a grand mansion. Its style is consistent, since instead of being the result of change and improvements by succeeding generations, the hall was an entirely new building erected in 1887, when the Cutlers had to give up their fourth hall to make room for Cannon Street Station. It is quietly comfortable in a sombre, panelled, nineteenth-century sort of way. All the lights were specially designed in wrought iron, a change from the crystal chandeliers more common in City Livery Companies, and of course there is plenty of stained glass, but that in the windows on the first floor landing is

Fishmongers Hall from London Bridge.
The Fishmongers have occupied this prime site overlooking the river since 1434, but have been a little too close to London Bridge for comfort. In 1827 they had to pull down their Renaissance Hall to make way for the new London Bridge and the present Hall was threatened again in 1968 when work on the new London Bridge was started. However, the construction of the bridge has now been successfully completed without disruption to the Fishmongers' Hall.

seventeenth century and comes from the old hall. The elephant, the Company symbol, like the Fishmongers' dolphin, is a ubiquitous ornament. Along the front of the exterior is a most remarkable terracotta frieze, a unique work of art wrought by a young boy called Creswick, who was discovered in a Cutler's workshop by John Ruskin. It is said to be the only existing, accurate, representation of the trade of cutlery as exercised in Victorian times and the faces of the figures on the frieze are those of Creswick's fellow-workers in Sheffield.

The Dyers and the Founders Halls are the last of the Victorian ones. Smaller and less ornate than the others, their interiors are more like the modern halls. In the Founders' case this is due to the fact that the inside was completely modernized in 1966. The Dyers' entrance hall is given a contemporary appearance by the swan paintings on the walls by Peter Scott.

The remaining halls have all been built this century, one in 1925, fifteen since the Second World War, and one is still on the drawing board. Although the halls themselves are not old the actual sites on which they stand, in the majority of cases, have been in the possession of the Companies a very long time. Since over half the Companies' halls are still situated on their original sites, the City has to a large extent been built around them. For this reason livery halls are often hard to find; in cul-de-sacs and within inner courtyards, they lurk undetected by the busy workers rushing past. An observant pedestrian can however spot them by the coat of arms over a doorway or a discreet brass plaque beside the door bell. Of course the size of the sites has been gradually whittled away as the price of property increased and the Companies needed money to improve their halls or replenish their resources. Gradually they sold off their extensive gardens and sweeping frontages till all that was left was the hall itself, squeezed between high office blocks – a relic of the past wrapped in tradition and Portland stone. The Grocers Company, for instance, in 1426 bought the house and garden of Lord Fitzwalter in Old Jewry for £213 6s. 8d. In 1798 they sold half their garden to the Bank of England for £20,000, and they have recently just sold off another small slice to finance the setting up of a new charity. The site of Grocers Hall is probably the most valuable, situated as it is within a stone's throw of the Mansion House, the Bank and the Royal Exchange.

Those who didn't sell, developed. Some Companies with land to spare took advantage of the expansion of commercial life and built shops and offices in their gardens and on any available space around their halls. As a result nowadays some of the most desirable letting accommodation in the City is owned by the Livery Companies. The whole of Throgmorton Avenue for

Livery Hall of the Carpenters Company, laid up for a livery dinner. The most remarkable feature of this room, in which twenty-seven different kinds of wood have been used, is the hanging ceiling, 'Honeycombed' with cedar hexagonals, floating beneath an upper ceiling of dark blue. A few years after the Hall was built a marquetry Tree of Life by Sir Charles Wheeler was added at the far end of the hall.

instance is shared between the Carpenters and the Drapers. The Leathersellers own the whole of St Helen's Place, the cul-de-sac off Bishopsgate where their hall is situated, an area of just under two acres.

When it came to rebuilding the wrecked halls after the war many Companies applied the principle of development to the hall itself. The compensation the Companies received for war damage was assessed on the value of the property at the time of its destruction. But the scarcity of men and materials, and the problems of planning permission delayed the actual rebuilding for ten or even twenty years after the payment of the compensation, by which time building costs had escalated and prices soared. The Companies could not afford therefore to rebuild in the style to which they were accustomed. So what they did was to build a hall with office premises to let. The office space was the bread and butter, the hall the meat in the middle. They mostly designed the outside of their buildings to look as much like a residence as possible, tucking the commercial side out of sight of the livery accommodation. It was not only the hard up Minor Companies who adopted this technique: some of the Great Twelve, like the Haberdashers, Clothworkers and even the Mercers are all getting income from letting office space incorporated within their halls.

The most recent developers are the Plaisterers, who, after losing their hall in 1940, had the site which they had owned for four hundred years compulsorily purchased in 1956. With determination they set about acquiring a new one, but it took fourteen years before they had found what they wanted with planning permission for the required scale of development. The Company has now built a splendid hall as part of a larger development including 50,000 square feet of lettable office space at Number One, London Wall, which was opened by the Lord Mayor in November 1972.

In contrast to the very contemporary way in which the Plaisterers went into the property business, the Bakers have retained an element of medieval trading in their arrangements. When they came to rebuild their third hall in 1962 they had a valuable site in Harp Lane, for which they had paid £20 in 1506, but not much money available to spend on building. They therefore leased the site on a ninety-nine year lease to Wates, who built a ten-storey building with hall premises and six floors of offices above. The Bakers retain the freehold of the original site and rent the hall premises at a peppercorn rent from Wates. The rent is paid in kind and consists of six loaves ceremoniously weighed on the old scales still in Bakers Hall and presented on Midsummer's Day. The loaves are baked by students of the

Plaisterers Hall development at Number One, London Wall. The main part of the development which was completed in November 1972, comprises 50,000 square feet of office space; on the right the little hexagonal tower leads to the livery suite beneath. The unsuspecting visitor entering through this simple brick entrance hall is completely unprepared for the Georgian grandeur of the hall interior, in complete contrast to the very modern exterior of the building (see page 102).

THIS WAS THE PARISH CHVRCH
OF ST OLAVE SILVER STREET
DESTROY'D BY THE DREADFVLL
FIRE IN THE YEAR 1666.

Ironmongers Hall from an inner courtyard. The Company's original Hall was in Fenchurch Street on a site purchased in 1457 by nineteen Ironmongers. They were one of a very few Companies not to lose their Hall in the Great Fire of 1666, but it was destroyed in a German air raid on 7th July 1917. The present Hall is a Tudor copy built in 1925 under the direction of Mr. Sydney Tatchell, CBE, Surveyor to the Company from 1921 to 1953.

Borough Polytechnique and the two best student bakers each year are given the freedom of the Bakers Company.

What really bedevils arrangements for rebuilding is the longevity of the Company itself. There is a danger that whatever decisions are made in regard to the financing of the hall, will be too short-sighted in the long run. Already some Companies are worrying what they will do in another hundred years when their new halls will be growing old gracefully, but the office accommodation surrounding them will be in need of redevelopment.

Apart from the problem of financing the rebuilding and of obtaining planning permission, the next question concerned what architectural style should be adopted. This also posed a dilemma. On the one hand the Companies wished to be true to their craft-guild traditions by encouraging modern designers and craftsmen, on the other hand the historic treasures they had rescued from earlier halls looked better in period settings. Could they be sure that contemporary architecture would withstand the judgement of future generations, or should they faithfully reproduce the styles which had passed the test of time?

The Ironmongers went wholeheartedly for reproduction. Any visitor to this hall might at first be fooled into thinking it was the oldest of them all, since it is a perfect copy of a Tudor mansion. It was in fact built in 1925 on a new site the Ironmongers obtained in 1922 after their old hall in Fenchurch Street had been hit by a German bomb in 1917. In fact the Company nearly lost their present hall again in 1966, when they were threatened with a compulsory purchase order. The plans for the new Museum of London included the Ironmongers' property, but after a long-drawn-out battle, the Company was able to obtain a decision from the Minister of Housing leaving the hall out of the scheme. The reason that the Ironmongers Hall looks so realistically Tudor is that so much of the work was done by hand. The bricks, the panelling, the intricate ironwork on doors and casement windows is all the work of individual craftsmen. Sydney Tatchell who designed the hall was determined to recapture the golden age of craftsmanship and to copy old designs as accurately as possible. Even the ceilings are modelled on genuine Elizabethan ones, such as that in the long gallery at Haddon Hall in Derbyshire.

Bestriding both horns of the dilemma is the Plaisterers Hall, with an ultra-modern exterior and neo-Georgian interior. The City of London Planning Authority wanted a contemporary building and the Company's architect John Davey of Ronald Ward and Partners felt that a Georgian framework was unsuitable for office accommodation. But the Plaisterers wanted a hall which would be a credit to the plastering trade. So the livery suite was built beneath a modern office block in a flamboyantly period style. The entrance hall leading from the exterior is a modern regular hexagon, finished inside and out with two-inch thick Whitwick facing bricks. The unsuspecting visitor entering through this simple brick tower is completely unprepared, therefore, for the Georgian grandeur of the interior of the hall. The first shock is the colour. The pastel shades of the Georgian period – blues, greens, rose and dove grey picked out in gold – are very different from the rather subdued colours of most livery halls. Then there is the brilliance of the massive chandeliers; the ones made for the great hall are twelve feet high and eight feet wide. Everything down to the specially woven rose-coloured Axminster carpet is a faithful copy of Robert Adam's eighteenth-century design. The ceilings and friezes are a triumph for the craft and 250 plasterers were employed on their elaboration. The great hall is the biggest of the livery banqueting halls. Strangely enough with the exception of the Merchant Taylors, which can hold up to three hundred, no other Company can cater for much more than two hundred. It therefore seems that the Plaisterers have set out to redress the balance, and already the hall has been described as 'the City's answer to the Connaught Rooms'. In the great hall the carpet is laid on a polished floor which can be used for dancing and a Hammond concert organ has been installed.

In the Carpenters Hall the mixture of ancient and modern is the other way round. The Victorian facade of the old hall still remains but inside the Carpenters have concentrated on contemporary design and the use of wood. The entrance hall, panelled in Elizabethan oak and hung with Tudor murals from the old hall, hints at the Company's medieval beginnings, but then gradually the design becomes more up to date until it reaches a peak of modernity in the banqueting hall. Here twenty-seven different kinds of woods are used to demonstrate the full range of the carpenter's art. At the far end a marquetry 'Tree of Life' by Sir Charles Wheeler complements the simple and modern design of the room. The most remarkable feature is the hanging ceiling, which is 'honeycombed' with cedar hexagonals edged with gold, floating beneath an upper ceiling of dark blue.

With the exception of the Grocers Hall, which was completed in November 1970 in a 'restrained contemporary style', all the rest of the halls have been rebuilt in a traditional way, but without attempting to receate exact replicas of a given period. The Clothworkers, Saddlers, Leathersellers, Barber-Surgeons, Butchers, Brewers, Haberdashers, Painter Stainers and Bakers have buildings which contrast with the towering modern office blocks around them. However skilfully designed and decorated a hall may be in the traditions of the past nothing can match the atmosphere that age bestows. So these Companies have tried various devices that might help to give their new halls a well-seasoned look.

Heraldic symbols provide a bit of colour and are used a great deal in the City today, particularly by the Livery Companies, whose armorial bearings go back to their early days of power in the fourteenth and fifteenth centuries. Students of heraldry will therefore find rich material for study in the many coats of arms

Cut-glass lustre and ormolu chandelier made in Russia for Catherine the Great and given by her to James Harris (later first Earl of Malmesbury) when he was Ambassador at St. Petersburg in the seventeen-eighties. The chandelier was given to the Skinners in 1950 by the sixth Earl of Malmesbury, Warden and subsequently Master of the Company, and it now hangs in the outer hall at Skinners Hall.

which embellish the exteriors and interiors of livery halls. The Haberdashers for instance have liberally decorated their modern hall in Staining Lane with the arms of the Company, the City, sovereigns who granted them charters and those of over forty members of the Company who have been Lord Mayor.

Panelling is almost obligatory in any livery hall and much original seventeenth- and eighteenth-century woodwork has been successfully transplanted. Nor does all panelling have to be old; in the Butchers' banqueting hall and luncheon room the walls are covered with Australian black bean and New Zealand southland beech, presented to them by their trade associates in the Commonwealth. Valuable stained glass from past ages has been successfully used to enhance new surroundings, but modern stained glass can be even more effective. The windows in the Bakers Hall designed by John Piper to commemorate the three fires which have destroyed the three previous Bakers Halls add a wonderfully dramatic touch of colour to their simple banqueting hall.

Gifts from past Masters can still help to furnish a hall, like the beautiful Flemish tapestries which enrich the marbled austerity of the Clothworkers' staircase; or a treasured relic from an old hall, like the Grocers' superb wrought-iron gates. These were painstakingly restored to their former magnificence and erected in the Company's new banqueting hall. Their presence there is somewhat bizarre, but of great sentimental value to the Grocers. The Barber-Surgeons Hall is decorated with some rather gruesome tools of the barbers' old trade—porcelain bleeding bowls, delftware pill slabs and sixteenth-century Fleems (bleeding instruments).

The Mercers have so much that is aged with which to embellish their hall that although it was built in 1958 it retains a lot of the character of a much older one. They are the only Company who still have their own chapel within the building, and in the ambulatory there is a very unusual stone carving. It is a full-length figure of Christ and was found by workmen in 1954 when the bombed site of the Mercers Hall was being cleared. It seems likely that the statue was carved prior to 1538, and that it was buried in that year under the floor of either the Mercers' own chapel or that of St Thomas of Acon. Red plush fabrics and darkened wood panelling give the hall an air of dignified masculinity, but the fine seventeenth- and eighteenth-century crystal chandeliers, together with the Grinling Gibbons carving, add a sense of style which cannot be achieved by contemporary good taste alone. The sense of history is heightened by the full-length portrait of Sir Thomas Gresham, painted in 1544, which hangs on the staircase. One of the wealthiest and most influential of the Mercers, Gresham built the Royal

Ornamental finial in the form of a lion on the seventeenth-century staircase in Vintners Hall. Arms are the seventeenth century royal arms of King Charles II.

Girdlers Hall in Basinghall Avenue. This is the Girdlers' third Hall. The first was built sometime in the first half of the fifteenth century and destroyed in the Great Fire of 1666. The second was completed in 1682 and destroyed in the great German raid on the night of Sunday 29th December, 1940. This one was built in the nineteen-sixties.

Exchange and also founded Gresham College. Ingenious outside lighting illuminates the Victorian stained glass windows, depicting Thomas à Becket, Richard II and Elizabeth I. One advantage of a modern hall is that it can make use of recent technical inventions. The air in the Mercers' banqueting hall is changed twelve times an hour and electrically operated shutters outside the hall windows can be operated simultaneously at the touch of a switch.

One hall which does not rely on relics from the past is the Girdlers which is a red-brick Queen-Anne-style hall built in the 1960s. It has no office premises to let and with its well-kept garden and colourful window boxes is rather like a charming country house which has strayed into the City by mistake. The informal elegance of the outside is reflected in the interior decoration. Some Companies leave the planning of their decor to a committee but the Girdlers' was the responsibility of one man. The Company left it all to a past Master whose taste and knowledge they completely trusted and who was unhampered by a lot of relics which had to be incorporated in the new surroundings. He therefore had a completely free hand to choose curtains, carpets, wallpaper and furniture which would all complement each other and create a well-balanced whole.

The Pewterers Hall, like the Girdlers, is more of a home than a hall, with no office premises to interfere with its singular detachment. A free-standing brick neo-Georgian building, it is a pigmy among the skyscrapers. The entire accommodation consists only of a livery room on the ground floor, a court room above, fifty feet by twenty-four, anterooms and cloak and robing rooms, a small office and a Beadle's flat. Unless there is a livery dinner or court meeting, the hall's tranquillity is therefore undisturbed by the hurly-burly of the commercial world outside.

One Company shares a hall with the parish of St Botolph. The nineteenth-century parish schoolroom of the Church of St Botolph was badly damaged in the war and neglected thereafter. In 1952 the Fanmakers restored and redecorated it in a manner appropriate to a City Company. The oak panelling dates back to 1726, the curtains are modelled on a very old Tudor design, and the arms of the Company are now depicted in a stained glass window. The Fanmakers have exclusive use of the hall on twenty-four days of the year and for the rest of the time it continues to serve the parishioners as a meeting place.

Obviously the high cost of obtaining land on which to build a hall in the City of London rules out the possibility of a new Livery Company ever aspiring to own one. However, the Honourable Company of Master Mariners has overcome the problem by converting a sloop and mooring it on the Thames by the Temple stairs. For a Company whose members are entirely composed of seamen it is both an appropriate and comfortable headquarters.

Salters Hall, which is still on the drawing board, promises to be uncompromisingly contemporary. It is being built in Fore Street off London Wall and is designed by Basil Spence. The Company looks forward to the day when it will be the proud possessor of a hall once more, which may be controversial but will certainly be remarkable, befitting the Salters' station as one of the Great Twelve Companies.

Chapter 3

Treasure

And I do hereby wish that my means were agreable to my Will, then should they record me a better benefactor.
From the Deed of Gift of Richard Weoley, 1644

A Livery Company is what the support of past members has made it, especially in the quantity and quality of its treasure. Since some of the wealthiest have been on the receiving end of bountiful benefaction for over five hundred years and are unaffected by death duties today, their inheritance is superb.

The greatest proportion of this inherited treasure is in pieces of silver or silver-gilt plate. Collecting valuable plate was the earliest form of banking and a glittering assortment of precious utensils on a rich man's table was an investment as well as an outward display of consequence. So the medieval benefactors left a piece of silver to enrich the feasts of their brethren, which could also be turned into hard cash when the need arose. It is only fairly recently that silver objects have been revered for their antiquity; in the past they were often melted down for cash or remodelling. But although collections today have been affected by financial pressures encountered in the course of those five centuries, and also by the desire of succeeding generations to improve on the designs of their predecessors, some of the finest secular pieces of plate in existence are still owned by the Livery Companies.

The early fraternities were mainly preoccupied with treasure in heaven and it was not until the end of the fifteenth century that several guilds began to build up a common stock of plate. By this time they had outgrown their purely religious purpose and their more prosperous members were helping them to lay up treasure upon earth. Often the first gifts were a modest spoon or a simple drinking cup. One of the Mercers' earliest treasures is a set of diamond-point spoons, given by Richard Whittington early in the fifteenth century. Among the Minor Companies spoons were often all their members could afford to give; the

The Venetian glass goblet with silver-gilt foot, dated about 1527, which was given to the Founders by Richard Weoley, who was Master of the Company in 1631. In his will Richard Weoley describes the goblet as 'my painted Drinking Glass, with the silver and gilt foot'.

first recorded items of any silver in the Turners Company do not appear until 1609 and consist of two silver and gilt spoons valued at 26s. 8d. Spoons were so useful a commodity to have put by for a rainy day that many Companies exacted them from newly elected freemen when they joined the guild. This practice stood the Coopers Company in good stead in 1664, when they found themselves short of £142 to pay their share of a forced loan to Charles II, and succeeded in raising the required amount by the sale of five wine cups and 354 spoons. The Goldsmiths have one of the very few complete sets of Apostle spoons in existence, made in 1626 and given them by George Lambert in the nineteenth century. But in addition to spoons the Companies were given drinking cups, gallon pots, basins and ewers, large silver salvers, goblets and salts in silver, silver-gilt or parcel gilt by their most prosperous members.

Gifts were entirely voluntary but the spirit of benefaction was complicated by many ulterior motives. Some liverymen did not want to be involved in the costly and time-consuming business of serving as Master or Warden and escaped their obligations in return for presenting their guild with a suitably impressive treasure. Thomas Seymour, for instance, was excused serving as Touchwarden and all other offices of the Goldsmiths Company after he presented them with a magnificent standing salt in 1693. This piece had been made for Queen Catherine of Braganza on her marriage to Charles II, but when she returned to Portugal after Charles' death she left it behind and Seymour subsequently bought it as a fitting gift to make his mark with the Goldsmiths. The Merchant Taylors, due to the reluctance of William Offley to serve as Master of the Company in 1590, are the richer for two parcel gilt basins and an ewer.

Others attempted to bribe the Wardens to overlook substandard workmanship. A fine Elizabethan salt in the possession of the Goldsmiths Company was given them by Simon Gibbon on St Bartholomew's Day 1632, after a search by Wardens of the Company for base metal in workshops throughout the City. The unworthy thought has subsequently crossed the minds of one or two Goldsmiths that Gibbon hoped so to dazzle the Wardens by this magnificent present that they would be blind to any traces of base metal in his workshop.

Even royalty has on occasions made a gesture of generosity to a favoured craft. The Barber-Surgeons seem to have done especially well from royal patronage and has no less than four pieces which were personal gifts from the Crown. One of the finest pre-Reformation objects in the City of London is the Barber-Surgeons' silver instrument case, which is believed to have been given them by Henry VIII when he became their

Gilt standing salt, made by order of the corporation of Portsmouth for presentation to Queen Catherine of Braganza on her arrival in England for her marriage to Charles II and later given to the Goldsmiths Company by Thomas Seymour in 1693.

patron in 1512. A gilt standing mazer with a cover was much admired by Pepys when he went to dine with the Barbers in 1662. 'Among other observations we drunk the King's Health out of a gilt cup given by Henry VIII to this Company, with bells hanging at it, which every man is to ring by shaking after he hath drunk up the whole cup.' The piece was a present from Henry VIII to celebrate the union of the Barbers with the Surgeons in 1540. Maybe with superb foresight the King was buying the goodwill of the Company on whom he would have to rely for blood letting and other remedies during his later years of ill-health. The Company also have a parcel gilt standing cup and cover given them by Charles II in 1676. It is known as the Oak Cup, as the stem is like a tree trunk and the bowl is embossed with oak branches and foliage from which hang four acorns. The fourth royal gift is a punch bowl or wine cistern given to the Barber-Surgeons by Queen Anne.

But the best reason for giving was affection for the Guild; and this feeling, common to the majority of benefactors, is charmingly expressed by Richard Weoley who gave the Founders in 1644 a beautiful Venetian glass goblet:

> and whereas I the said Richard Weoley, for 34 years have been a Member of the Livery of the Company of Founders, of the City of London, from whom I always have good respect and observation ever showed to me in that time aforesaid, in requital whereof I give and bequeath unto the said Company my painted Drinking Glass, with the silver and gilt foot, which by relation was brought from Bullen (Boulogne) out of France, at the time when Henry the VIII King of England had that place yielded unto him; this Glass being part of the pillage then taken by a Yeoman of the Crown, and hath remained in one and the same family to this day. . . . And I do hereby wish that my means were agreable to my Will, then should they record me a better Benefactor. And I shall ever wish the whole Body may ever live in Unity, Concord and Brotherly Love, which is pleasing to God and Man. Even thus the God of Heaven Bless them all—Amen.

But all was not uninterrupted acquisition. What came as gifts disappeared by confiscation, poverty or fire. The Crown was a far more rapacious taker than generous giver. During the time of the Reformation the levies imposed by Henry VIII were beyond the means of many Companies, who had to sell their silver. The Armourers to meet the King's demands sold everything they had except one little stoneware jar, which was not considered of any value. This was a silvermounted, brown stoneware Owl Pot, bequeathed them in 1537 by Julyan Vyneyard, widow of William Vyneyard, which is now of great value as the oldest item in their collection. The Fishmongers had to

Gilt standing salt, dated 1576. It is the finest surviving example of its kind and was presented to the Goldsmiths Company on St. Bartholomew's Day 1632, by Simon Gibbon, after a search through the City for wares of base metal.

pay £18,744 to the Royal Exchequer to redeem their confiscated property and consequently all their silver was melted down. In the seventeenth century the expense of the Civil War took its toll of the silver collections in the City. Goldsmiths Hall was turned into the Parliamentarian exchequer and all the Companies had to bring their quota to be melted down into coin to pay Cromwell's soldiers.

But it was, of course, the Great Fire of 1666 which was the most terrible melting pot of all. Most of the silver not actually reduced to a molten mass by the flames had to be sacrificed afterwards to pay for rebuilding. The Companies who were great City landlords also had to sell silver to make up for the income they lost from their properties. In those days most tenants had rebuilding leases and were responsible for rebuilding the properties after the frequent fires. But it was not until property had been rebuilt that tenants started paying rent again. The decision taken by the Court of the Goldsmiths, recorded in their Minutes of 5 July 1667, was similar to that forced upon many of the Great Twelve by the disaster:

> In consideration of the many urgent and pressing occasions of the company, for the raising of money for their present service, and more especially for that of repairing the hall. And that the company have no occasion to make use of their plate nor place convenient where the same may be secured. It is at this court agreed, that all, or at least such part thereof as is not serviceable shall be sold. Yet with such respect to the benefactors' gifts, as that such as shall be parted with, the coats of arms and other inscriptions may be carefully taken and the same recorded in the company's court books. In order that such amount of plate may be restored and made again, when the company shall be thereunto enabled.

Fate played its part in preserving some treasure and occasionally a Minor Company by a lucky chance was able to save its early plate and so today has an unexpectedly good collection. The Innholders, for instance, have a wealth of pre-fire silver because in July 1665 the Company's plate for some reason was transferred to the home of the Master, which was The Ram at Smithfield. It was still there a year later when the Innholders Hall was burnt to the ground and consequently it escaped the flames. The Armourers and Brasiers have many beautiful early drinking vessels which were saved from the melting pot during the Civil War because the Armourers were of Royalist sympathies. Members of their Court took the precious silver cups to their respective homes and buried them in their gardens out of sight of Cromwell's money-raising officers. On Charles II's return the Armourers' cups all came out of hiding and every one was returned to Armourers Hall.

Gilt standing mazer, surmounted by the Tudor arms, and dated 1523. It bears the inscription inside the cover, 'Lest it should remain unknown to posterity this is of the munificence of King Henry—John Knight, Principal Surgeon to the King, 1678.' The cup was given to the Company by Henry VIII in 1540 on the occasion of the union of the Barbers with the Surgeons. In 1649 it was sold but was bought by Edward Arris who gave it back to the Company.

The plate considered most dispensable was the unfashionable plate dating from before the Civil War, so it was the earliest pieces which were melted down after the Great Fire. The smaller, more serviceable items such as drinking cups were the last to go. Drinking vessels abound in City collections and there were many very different shaped cups which had a practical as well as an artistic purpose. Mazers and tazzas were wide shallow bowls so designed that the sediment in the rough wine of the time would sink to the bottom of the cups. A mazer was a wooden bowl elegantly finished with a silver rim and central boss and a tazza was a saucer-shaped silver bowl on a stand. Tumbler cups for travelling were unadorned and rounded to fit into each other. In the sixteenth century the exotic coconuts brought back from overseas were regarded with such wonder that even their shells were considered precious enough to be made into impressive objects for display. The Armourers and Ironmongers each have a fine coconut cup made at the beginning of the sixteenth century. The Grocers' earliest piece is a 1580 coconut cup and the Cooks also have an Elizabethan coconut cup. Beakers, wine cups and goblets are the treasured possessions of many Companies for their age and simple beauty, but best of all are the standing cups and covers.

These were the élite of drinking vessels and elaborate works of art. When all else had to be melted down for cash, the guilds still clung tenaciously to their magnificent standing cups, many of which are therefore still in their collections today. Probably the oldest is the Armourers' Richmond Cup, presented to the Company in 1547 by John Richmond, Master 1547–8. It is unmarked but thought to have been made in the 1480s. The Mercers' magnificent Leigh Cup of 1499 was presented to the Company by Sir Thomas Leigh in 1571. The Goldsmiths' gilt and crystal Bowes Cup, given to them by Sir Martin Bowes, Prime Warden in 1558, is traditionally believed to have been drunk from by Queen Elizabeth I at her coronation banquet. The Drapers Lambard Cup also has Elizabethan connections. It bears the royal arms, together with the Drapers' arms and those of Sir William Cordelle, Master of the Rolls, and is dated 1578. It was presented to the Company by William Lambard, the antiquary. These are some of the oldest and most magnificent but there are many more belonging to other Companies. The Armourers have a number of sixteenth-century standing cups of great beauty as well as the Richmond Cup. The Carpenters and Cutlers have some very beautiful steeple cups, a seventeenth-century development so called because the finial of the cover is shaped like the long tapering spire of a steeple.

Unique to the Vintners is their wager cup, which is marked 1680. These cups were well known in Holland as drinking

French silver-gilt Clock-salt, probably made in Paris between 1530 and 1535. It is believed to have been a present to Henry VIII from the French King Francis I and was listed in the Tudor inventories. When the salt was bought by the Goldsmiths in 1968 it was no longer in its original condition having suffered alterations in the 18th and 19th centuries. The Goldsmiths decided to try to restore it to its original appearance. The restoration work included removing a nineteenth century clock on the summit and replacing it with a crystal salt container and lid more in keeping with the genuinely Tudor body.

vessels in the late seventeenth century, but examples in England were rare. Although there are many replicas the Vintners have the only genuine one of that period in the City. The cup takes the form of a milkmaid dressed in the style of the mid-seventeenth century, whose petticoat forms the cup. Above her head she holds a smaller cup on a swivel. According to tradition every liveryman of the Vintners Company was required to drink prosperity to the Company from the larger vessel and then the health of the Master from the smaller, without spilling the contents. A great deal of money has been hazarded on the successful completion of this difficult feat—hence the name of the cup.

At first gifts tended to be personal possessions of the donor and might have been in private use for some time before being bequeathed to a guild; but as time went on Companies acquired pieces which were far too grand ever to have been used domestically. The Mercers' Wagon and Tun—a flamboyant piece of ingenious workmanship made in Breslau in the early sixteenth century and presented to them by William Birde in 1533—is very impressive. It is an elaborately chased and engraved wagon on four wheels in the middle of which is poised a barrel which contained scented water. This remarkable rosewater dish moved along the table by an internal mechanism and people dining with the Mercers supposedly washed their fingers very quickly with rosewater from the barrel as it perambulated past them. It is ornamented with silver and enamelled figures and the wagon is crowned by an eagle on a globe. The majority of the Great Twelve have imposing salts with which to decorate their tables, although they are no longer used to emphasize the social niceties. Although most salts were made before the Restoration, some of the Minor Companies, like the Upholders, the Tin Plate Workers, the Wax-Chandlers, Glovers and Needlemakers, keep up appearances at their dinners with some late seventeenth-century masterpieces.

There is no shortage of late seventeenth-century plate in the City. After the Companies had recovered from the Great Fire they began slowly to replace their lost possessions. The reaction to the years of Puritan rule showed itself artistically in extravagant ornamentation. Outsize ceremonial pieces, ewers and basins, giant wine cisterns and tankards and standing cups became popular. The Clothworkers are proud of their gift from Samuel Pepys, one-time Master of the Company, who presented them with an elaborate standing cup, basin and ewer in 1677. These are fairly typical of the sort of items being made at the time, but the engraving is of outstanding quality. Great silver punch bowls called montieths became popular because of their suitability as a present of obviously solid worth. Candlesticks and candelabra ousted spoons as useful assets to acquire.

Of course there were certain things peculiar to a Livery Company, such as the Beadles' staffheads, which had always been specially made. These important pieces of official insignia are interesting individual works of art and at least one—the Weavers'—is very old. This is a simple wooden staffhead made in about 1500 with a silver-gilt mount at each end, bearing the arms and crown of the Weavers. Most of the others were made later in silver or silver-gilt and feature the Company's symbol or an elaborate representation of the arms of the Company. The Mercers for instance have a pair of maces made in 1679 for £29 5s. which are cast solid and are in the form of a crowned maiden, the symbol of the Company. The Cutlers' staffhead is surmounted by a silver elephant and castle and the Blacksmiths' embodies trade symbolism in the shape of a hammer crowned with the Company arms and a phoenix rising from the flames.

In the eighteenth and nineteenth centuries, while the poorer Companies were selling what little plate they had left to try to

Silver-gilt salt and wine barrel made in Breslau in the early sixteenth century. The salt is enamelled with the arms of the City of London and of the Mercers Company. The barrel is normally placed on the carriage of the wagon. It rests on a foliated knob upon a lozenge pedestal with an oval foot, on which are four bosses of blue and green enamel on silver. (See opposite.)

keep going, the wealthier were acquiring pieces on a massive scale. They were not, however, allowed to enjoy the fruits of their consolidated positions entirely unmolested and were fairly hard hit by an Act of Parliament in 1756 imposing a heavy tax on antique silver and gold. Companies like the Apothecaries decided to sell 'all such as is useless and unfashionable', which unfortunately included two silver-gilt sixteenth-century 'college' cups which they would have been very pleased to see in their collection today. However, the wealthier Companies with money coming in from their valuable properties in the City were able to withstand such minor attacks, and even to replace some of the silver they had lost.

Standing cups and covers were still proliferating and the Pewterers have a very fine example of one made in 1705, which has

all the best characteristics of the Queen Anne period. One of the most favoured craftsmen of the eighteenth century was a second generation Huguenot called Paul de Lamerie and the City abounds with examples of his work. Sometimes he let his genius for applied decoration carry him a little too far, as with the two-handled cup and cover with its horribly lifelike serpent handles which he made in 1737 for Henry, fourth Baron Maynard, and was presented to the Fishmongers in 1949. However, Lamerie's gilt ewer and basin, commissioned by the Goldsmiths in 1740 to replace some of their plate previously melted down, are truly magnificent examples of his work. Some of the later two-handled cups and covers became so large and important that they looked more like a cross between a soup tureen and a tankard. But the revival of the loving cup ceremony at livery dinners in the nineteenth century increased their popularity and there are probably more standing cups and covers in the Companies' collections than any other single items of plate.

Towards the end of the nineteenth century more and more of the plate the Companies acquired was already old, and this trend has continued into the twentieth. Not every Company can match the contribution of the Goldsmiths who by their intervention saved a valuable Tudor clock salt from going abroad. This salt was made in Paris in 1530 and was a gift to Henry VIII from Francis I of France. The piece was listed in the Tudor inventories of Royal Plate and last appears amongst the royal possessions in the inventory drawn up in 1649 for Oliver Cromwell where a marginal note indicates that it was sold to a 'Mr Smith'. In 1968 its nineteenth-century additions, which included a clock on its summit, fooled a leading firm of London auctioneers into entering it in a sale of clocks and so it was not recognized for the exceptional Tudor salt that it was. It went for a paltry sum, but when the importance of the piece was discovered there was trouble with the export licence. The Goldsmiths were then given the chance to buy it and keep it in the country.

Equally esoteric but a little more humble is the Watermen's collection of silver badges won by apprentices in the various regattas held on the river during the nineteenth century. From time to time such badges appear in the salerooms and when the Company can afford to do so they add another badge to their collection. Sometimes pieces originally commissioned by a Company reappear in a saleroom, and are bought back again. The Skinners for instance have recently purchased a lovely gold snuff box bearing the Skinners' arms, which was presented by the Company to Admiral the Earl Howe, when he was made an Honorary Freeman of the Company.

Magnificent gilt standing cup and cover enriched with translucent enamel dated 1499. Inscribed in modern silver lettering reserved against a blue enamelled ground: 'To elect the Master of the Mercerie hither am I sent and by Sir Thomas Leigh for the same entent.' It was bequeathed by Sir Thomas Leigh to the Mercers Company in 1571. (Opposite.)

Armourers and Brasiers' standing cup and cover made about the end of the fifteenth century. It was presented to the Armourers Company by John Richmond, Master in 1547-58 and is inscribed: 'Pra for Iohn Richemund Ientylman Cetesin and Armerar of Loundone and Eme and Iesabell his wyves.' (Pray for John Richmond gentleman citizen and armourer of London and Ame and Isobel his wives). (P.88.)

Gilt cup and cover by Paul de Lamerie dated 1737. The whole surface is finely embossed and chased in shellwork, scales and fish-like forms in high relief. The handles are formed as the bodies of snakes, the heads of which emerge from another part of the bowl. In spite of this, the cup was not originally made for the Fishmongers Company, and was given to them by Sir Harold Wernher in 1949.

An early sixteenth-century coconut cup which was given to the Ironmongers by 'Master Harre Sturgeon'. Coconuts were considered such rare and exotic fruits when they first appeared in England that the shells were preserved and fashioned into beautiful drinking vessels. (P.89.)

The Companies are still maintaining their role as patrons of young silversmiths and a certain amount of new work has been commissioned by various Companies. Naturally, with their close association with the trade, the Goldsmiths are in the lead. One of the most unusual modern works of art is a Narwhal Tusk balance designed by Louis Osman, commissioned for the Goldsmiths by Lord Runciman in 1963 as a Prime Warden's gift. This four-foot nine and a half inch whale's tusk is mounted in rose quartz and balanced on a wish-bone of silver-gilt. A movable rider, formed by a delicate viscount's coronet in gold, baroque pearls and baguette sapphires, acts as the balance which keeps the tusk delicately poised on the horizontal. The Old Bancroftians Association commissioned in 1964 a modern salt by Gerald Whiles which they presented to the Drapers Company to commemorate the granting of the Company's first charter. The Painter Stainers commissioned Leslie Durbin to design a four-branch silver candelabrum, featuring the phoenix and flames of the Company's crest, to replace some Elizabethan spoons and Charles II wine cups which had been melted down when the Company needed the money.

Although benefactors concentrated mostly on plate, partly for its investment potential and partly for its durability, they did not do so to the exclusion of all else. The Grocers, the Vintners and the Bakers have fine collections of glass bequeathed to them by members of their Companies and added to from time to time. Certain aspects of a Livery Company's life are enhanced by the grandeur of presentations made by liverymen through the centuries. The Master, for instance, needs a chair of throne-like importance from which to preside during his year's reign. Many magnificent Masters' chairs unfortunately have not survived to the present day, but the Armourers have one which they believe must at one time have belonged to Francis Drake for it has the initials F.D. and the date 1584 carved upon it. The Framework Knitters have an impressive 1670 chair made of carved wood with an elaborate gilt decoration, which is now in the Guildhall Museum. The Watermen have an 1800 Sheraton chair which they lent for a time to the Victoria and Albert Museum.

The annual election of the Master and other officials of a Company necessitates a ballot box and there are some lovely hand-carved wooden ones. The most colourful and elaborate, however, is undoubtedly the Saddlers', which was originally made for the East India Company in 1619. It is intricately painted and inlaid, in the Italian chinoiserie style of the sixteenth century. On the front of the box are painted the arms of James I and of the East India Company.

Although some collections for the poor were taken on large silver almsdishes, a few Companies used wooden boxes. The Coachmakers and Coach Harness Makers have a carved wooden poor box with full-length figures at each corner, the front two supporting drapery which bears the names of the Master and Wardens in 1680 when it was made. The Glass Sellers have a walnut poor box, inlaid with floral marquetry in various woods, the gift of John Green in 1690.

Although the valuable plate is now secreted in sophisticated safes, some Companies still retain their original strong boxes for their own sake. These fine iron chests were both attractive and, with a combination of elaborate locks which thieves found very hard to crack, impregnable. The Dyers' Armada chest, for maximum security, had three different locks and a key was kept

Gilt steeple cup made in 1611 and given to the Carpenters by John Reeve. One of a set of three steeple cups owned by the Carpenters and so called because the finial on the lid of the cup is in the shape of a steeple. This particular one is the Master's Cup and has a gilt Roman warrior on the finial of the cover.

Modern salt designed by Gerald Whiles made by William Comyns Ltd in 1964. It was given to the Drapers by the Old Bancroftians Association to celebrate the sexcentenary of the Company's first charter. (P.92.)

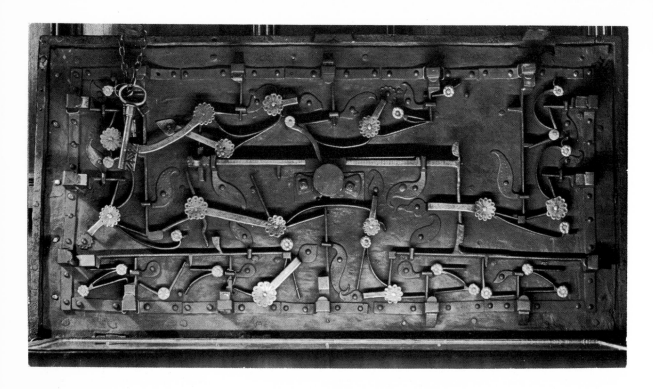

for each lock by a different Warden. It took six men to lift it even when empty and a triumvirate of Wardens to open it. The Vintners' chest has no less than thirteen locks in the lid, but they are all operated by the turn of a single key.

Fabric is far more fragile than furniture, yet the Companies have some beautiful examples of four-hundred-year-old needlework still in a fine state of preservation. The most remarkable are the funeral palls. In early days people were buried without a coffin and the corpse was carried on a bier covered by a hearse cloth. The fraternities had communal cloths of great beauty, which all members had the right to use for their burial. The magnificence of a guild's funeral pall was an outward sign of its consequence as well as a deep mark of respect for the dead, and these state hearse cloths were among the most treasured of their early possessions. Made of costly velvet, the borders were intricately embroidered in gold and coloured silks and depicted scenes from the craft of the guild interspersed with those of death. The Brewers, Saddlers, Merchant Taylors, Ironmongers, Vintners and Fishmongers still have remarkably beautiful funeral palls dating from the end of the fifteenth century.

There are also tapestries showing the best of the fifteenth, eighteenth and twentieth centuries. The Vintners have a rare early Flemish tapestry dated 1466 hanging in their hall. It depicts St Martin, the Company's patron saint, dividing his

A fine example of an early mazer, dating about 1460, belonging to the Goldsmiths Company. A mazer was a shallow wooden drinking bowl of maple (from which the name is derived). The shape of the bowl encouraged the sediment in the rough wine to settle on the bottom and give the drinker a clearer taste. In rich households these bowls were elaborated with silver or gilt decoration—as is this one, which has a silver gilt rim with gothic lettering.

cloak with a beggar and St Dunstan surprised at mass by hearing angels. Its dimensions indicate that it was intended as an altar hanging and at one time it is believed to have been at Canterbury. In the Drapers' court room hang two magnificent Gobelin tapestries which were made in the last years of Louis xv's reign. They are two of a set of four bought by the Drapers in 1881. The Grocers' new reception room is dominated by three dramatic modern tapestries, designed by John Piper, in brilliant colours symbolizing the spice trade of the Company.

The Girdlers have a rare Indian carpet which was made in the royal factory of Lahore in 1632. It is knotted by hand throughout in wools of various colours and in the centre bears the Company's crest and arms together with those of Robert Bell, the donor. One of the founders of the East India Company, Bell commissioned the carpet on one of his many trips to India, but he was a somewhat adventurous trader and there is some doubt as to whether he ever actually paid for it. The carpet had a very narrow escape during the last war. It had been placed for safety in an asbestos case in the basement strongroom of the Girdlers Hall, but the Master during 1940 had it removed to the vaults of the Westminster Bank in Lothbury. Ten days later the hall was ablaze and the heat of the basement was so intense that for five days no one could enter it. Asbestos would have been no protection in such a glowing inferno and had the carpet still been in the hall it would certainly have been reduced to charred thread.

Banners and pennants carried by the Companies in processions provide scope for elaborate embroidery. The Broderers have a four-foot by three-foot banner, embroidered with the Company's arms in gold and silver coloured thread, which is a fine example of their craft. In the dark Victorian banqueting hall of the Cutlers, protected by a shield of glass, is a great long banner hanging right across one end. This was a land banner carried in the Lord Mayor's procession of Alderman Bridgen in 1763. The silk is so old that were it to be exposed to the air it would soon crumble away to dust.

The Livery Companies possess the largest number of royal portraits in the country, but the great proportion are the work of minor artists and their collections are more notable for quantity than quality. One of the most famous is the Barber-Surgeons' Holbein, showing Henry VIII presenting the charter uniting the Barbers with the Surgeons, painted in 1542. This valuable picture spent the war years buried in a coal mine in Aberystwyth out of reach of German bombs. There are, of course, one or two pictures by famous artists which are not royal portraits. One such is the Merchant Taylors' Brueghel. It is a Flemish festival scene painted by Jan Brueghel I and presented to the Company in 1877. The Grocers have a Gainsborough, but sadly a second Gainsborough was destroyed in the 1965 fire. The Fishmongers have two full-length Romneys, and a second Annigoni portrait of the Duke of Edinburgh as well as the better known portrait by the same artist of the Queen. The Painter Stainers, as might be expected, have many pictures painted by former liverymen, such as Sir John Thornhill, a past Master of the Company. They also have two contemporary royal portraits, one of the Queen Mother by Sir Gerald Kelly and one of Prince Charles by Leonard Boden.

Some Companies have been able, particularly in the last century, to build up a collection of treasured examples of the work of their craft. Stored away in the Innholders Hall is a collection of unusual baskets belonging to the Basketmakers Company. This includes a collection of miniature baskets made in Madeira, which were presented to the Company by the Princess Royal in 1952 when she was made an honorary freewoman of the Company. They were collected by her brother the Duke of Kent, who gave his collection to his mother Queen Mary. Some other items are very much older and include pieces of unique early basket work. A piece of an ancient Egyptian shabti basket from the eleventh dynasty (2778–65 BC) was given to the Basketmakers by Lord William Cecil in 1915. The shabtis were the little people whom the ancient Egyptians believed accompanied Egyptian royal spirits in the underworld. Little baskets containing food for the shabtis were therefore put into the mummy cases of members of the royal household to sustain them.

The Pewterers have a display in their hall of early pewter including thirteenth-century stemmed pewter spoons and the earliest known English pewter flagon. Among the armour at Armourers Hall is a magnificent suit of elaborately wrought field armour which was made for Sir Henry Lee by Jacob Halder about 1587. Sir Henry was Master of the Queen's Armouries and Champion to Queen Elizabeth I. Part of the intricate decoration on this suit are the intertwined letters A.V. which were the initials of Anne Vavasour, the gallant knight's mistress.

At the Guildhall there are remarkable collections on display belonging to Livery Companies. One is the Spence collection of gloves, one of the finest of its kind in the world, which was presented by Robert Spence to the Glovemakers Company in 1959. Another is the Clockmakers' fascinating clock collection housed in the Guildhall library. For a period of some hundred years after the Clockmakers Company received its first charter in 1631, English clockmakers were the best in the world. The collection includes fine examples of such pioneers in precision timekeeping as the Harrison brothers, notably the long case clock made in 1728 by the younger Harrison which worked silently, never required oiling and twenty-one years after it was made was recorded as never having varied more than a second a month. The collection ranges from astrological clocks to the watch made by the first Master of the Company and a bizarre Mary Queen of Scots skull watch.

The Fanmakers have a collection of beautiful fans which they have collected this century. One of their treasured possessions is a plain chicken skin fan autographed with a number of royal signatures, collected on occasions when the Company has presented a fan to a royal bride.

The Makers of Playing Cards had a comprehensive collection of old playing cards which they presented to the Guildhall Museum in 1907. There are cards with full-length pictures on the court cards, hand-made before Thomas de la Rue received a patent in 1832 to print cards by machinery. Every year the

Playing Card Makers prepare a special pack for the exclusive use of their members, with the design on the back commemorating some notable event during the year and the portrait of the Master on the ace of spades. Every sort of significant event from royal jubilees to outbreaks of war has been pictorially recorded on the backs of a long line of special cards. There is no doubt that these unique treasures enhance the appeal of the Livery Companies. Through the generosity of past members they have been enriched with an abundance of material assets which enable them to put on a very splendid show. The gold and silver for their tables, beautiful furniture, rich fixtures and fittings for their halls and fragile relics of past pageantry which they have inherited and collected provide a colourful setting for their activities. So that today, when so little that glisters is really gold, the life-style of a Livery Company is very impressive.

Vintners' tapestry, dated 1466, depicting in one half the legend of St. Martin, patron saint of the Vintners, dividing his cloak with a beggar, and in the other St. Dunstan, patron saint of the Goldsmiths, surprised while taking mass by the singing of angels.

Lithograph published in 1830 satirising the over indulgence frequently to be found at City dinners in the nineteenth century.

Chapter 4

Feasting

As you love to see life in all its modes, if you have a mind to go you can come at 2 o'clock. The blackguards dine an hour later.
From SIR JOSHUA REYNOLDS' invitation to Boswell to come as his guest to dinner with the Painter Stainers Company.

Of the many roles Livery Companies play that of host is the most familiar. Their reputation for sumptuous feasting is something they prefer to play down as they feel it is such a small part of their overall activities. But they agree that in the quality of their surroundings, as well as the food and drink, livery dinners are hard to beat. Though the quantity consumed has been greatly reduced, the ritual which accompanies the meal has been preserved and even elaborated, so that the eating of dinner is transformed into a consummate art.

The earliest dinners took place in taverns when the members of the fraternities used to enjoy each other's company before they even acquired halls. This tradition of fellowship is a very important aspect of feasting today. A glance at any list of names at a livery dinner reveals that many of the guests come from other Companies. Liverymen can, of course, bring a guest once a year, or in some Companies every two or three years; usually one or two distinguished outsiders are also included; and occasionally there are important foreigners on a visit to London whom a Livery Company sometimes entertains to assist with government hospitality. However, the hard core of guests invited tend to be from within the fold – Masters, Wardens or Clerks of other Companies. Thus after some years a liveryman will tend to know many of the leaders from the other guilds. When he goes to Guildhall each year to vote for the Lord Mayor he will not be voting for a stranger but for a man he has dined with, heard speak and maybe even have sat next to on occasions during the past years. A tremendous bond of fellowship exists between the Livery Companies, cemented by two or three centuries of dining together, which helps them to present a united front today.

The Great Hall of the Plaisterers Company is the largest of any Livery Hall and seats between 300 and 350. The massive chandeliers, twelve foot high and eight foot wide, were specially made for the room and the elaborately decorated plaster work on ceilings and friezes is all hand done to show what modern plasterers can do.

Of course dinners vary enormously in impact from Company to Company. Some of the minor ones, who have to pay for their dinners, borrow the halls and even the plate of their more fortunate brethren, are little more than rather special dining clubs; whereas the greater have an ambience of wealth and ancient heritage which makes eating dinner there an impressive experience.

Although Companies vary in the extra flourishes in the art of dining, rosewater dishes, loving cups and snuff boxes are some traditional embellishments many, though not all, employ. The rosewater dish was an earlier sort of finger bowl, a costly silver or silver-gilt receptacle containing sweetly scented water. In earlier times after a meal eaten with their fingers, the guests needed to wash away the sticky mess from face and hands, so a dish of scented water was passed round the table after the third course. Now, although its presence is less pertinent than before, it is still passed round the table after the pudding course has been cleared away. The correct procedure is for the glasses to be pushed into the middle and the rosewater dish to be handed from guest to guest along the table. This method arises less from etiquette than from good sense, since with such a large and shallow dish, there is a very real danger that if passed from hand to hand, any man with a weak or unsteady hold could easily empty its contents into the lap of his unfortunate neighbour.

The loving cup ceremony is said to derive from the Saxon habit of passing round a drinking cup at parties as a token of goodwill, or from the wassail bowls of the Saxon monasteries, or from the Vikings who used to pledge each other across the table. Whatever its derivation, it is a popular ceremony with Livery Companies. The ceremony varies in detail from Company to Company. The Mercers Company for instance pass the cup to and fro across the table, though most of the others pass it along. The Turners adhere to the Saxon tradition of wassailing. They have a very fine seventeenth-century lignum wassail bowl, which at the appropriate moment the Clerk lifts up, and salutes the Master with an old English festive cry: 'Master–Wass Heil', and the Master replies: 'Drink Heil'. The Clerk then processes with the wassail bowl, followed by two Wardens carrying loving cups to where the Master sits, and he then fills the loving cups from the wooden wassail bowl.

It is part of the tradition that there should be three people standing up at one time, one of whom is drinking. This stems from the unsporting tendency of our forefathers to slay an enemy if they could take advantage of him while his head was buried in his drinking cup. After this fate overtook Edward the Martyr at Corfe Castle in 978, Oslac the Royal Cupbearer ruled that drinking horns and cups should be fitted with lids, and further that he who offered the cup must remove the lid with his dagger hand. Later it became the custom of a third person to stand behind the drinker to protect him from the rear. Many Companies have printed instructions for their liverymen on the drinking procedure, in order to avoid too many people bobbing up and down, unsure when they should be sitting, when protecting their companions' rear from enemy attack and when actually drinking.

The loving cups– usually two to the Master's table and one or

Gilt standing cup and cover dated 1578, is engraved with the arms of Queen Elizabeth I, the Drapers Company and Sir William Cordelle, Master of the Rolls. It was the gift to the Drapers from William Lambarde, the antiquary, in 1578, and is inscribed with the words: 'A Proctour for the poore am I & Remember theim before Thow dye 1578.'

two to each of the others—are passed round after grace has been said, or more often sung, at the dessert stage. What is actually in them is a modern version of the old medieval drink of hippocras, and each Company has its own recipe. Usually it is a mixture of wine laced with brandy, with cinnamon and lemon rind boiled in syrup. Wine in the Middle Ages was often sour or acid and in order to make it palatable it was mixed with herbs, sugar and honey, then filtered. The name hippocras derived from the sleeves of the alchemists which were used for filtering.

Apart from possible confusion over the loving cup, the unwary guest at the Clothworkers Company may also be a little perplexed when offered a tray of drinks and asked whether he drinks with Alderman or Lady Cooper. What he is being offered is a choice between gin and brandy. In the 1600s Alderman Cooper dropped dead after being rather well wined and dined by the Company. His widow, Lady Cooper, attributed his demise to too much brandy, and so provided the Company with gin in the hope that it would be drunk instead.

In some twenty per cent of Companies snuff boxes are still passed round with the cigars, cigarettes, coffee and liqueurs after the loyal toast. In the Tobacco Pipe Makers and Tobacco Blenders Company a special ceremony has been devised around the granting of permission to smoke. The Clerk walks up to the Master carrying a smoking cap. The Master puts the cap on his head, bows to the right, the centre and to the left, then takes it off and puts it on a stand in front of him, which is a signal that the Company may smoke.

An additional embellishment to most livery dinners is the music. Just as in the Middle Ages no banquet was complete without musicians and a wandering minstrel, so today every livery dinner has its complement of singers and sometimes a string instrument or two. A musicians' gallery is the ideal place for such performers and some of the modern halls include a more spacious imitation of the galleries of the past. The original musicians' galleries, which still exist in a few of the older halls, are narrow and insecure and the modern musician cannot always be persuaded to scramble up the rickety stairs and fiddle in the precarious perch they provide.

The majority of Companies play safe with singers, and extracts from Gilbert and Sullivan figure prominently in the repertoire. When a Company has a Master with a more imaginative approach to entertainment, occasionally more ambitious productions are attempted. The entertainment has, however, to compete with the speeches for the amount of time available. Since most liverymen nowadays sit down at seven o'clock in the

evening and expect to be homeward bound not long after half past ten, only about twenty minutes is allowed for theatrical endeavour. The Grocers Company recently experimented with some extracts of Restoration comedy performed by the Guild-hall School of Drama and Music at their Restoration Feast in May. One Company even had a conjuror, who sawed the Master in half and presented him with a certificate afterwards to prove it.

Some dinners are presented with such pageantry that they need no additional entertainers—like the boar's head feasts, celebrated by the Cutlers, Armourers and Carpenters Companies. A typical boar's head dinner as eaten in the Cutlers Hall just before Christmas would begin quite conventionally with turtle soup, river trout, wing of chicken in Chablis with peas and potatoes, and a lime sorbet. Then a trumpet sounds and a solemn little procession enters in full regalia led by the Beadle carrying his sixteenth-century staff; he is followed by the two trumpeters, the mustard pot carried by a page, then two chefs bearing on their shoulders the boar's head, garnished with rosemary, closely followed by the carver, with his knife and fork, two choir boys each carrying a lantern, the alto singer, the tenor singer, the bass singers, a choir boy carrying a torch and the chaplain at the rear. The carving of the boar's head is carried out to an accompaniment of the Boar's Head Carol, rendered by the choir. The cooking is a complicated business. An eighteenth-century recipe describes how the head must first be singed at the fire and rubbed with a piece of brick to take off the hair:

> then scrape it with a knife, and clean it well; when this is done bone it and cut out the two jaw-bones, and cut off the snout; slit it underneath, so that it may stick to the skin on top, and take away the brain and tongue; then take up salt upon the point of a knife, and cause it to penetrate through all the parts of the flesh; put the head together again, and wrap it up in a napkin and tie it; then put it into a large kettle of water made hot, with some leaf-fat of a hog's belly, two bay-leaves, all sorts of fine herbs, coriander and anniseeds, some salt, nutmeg and cloves beaten, some rosemary and an onion; when it is half-boiled, pour in a quart of good wine, and keep it boiling for twelve hours. You may also boil the tongue, with the same liquor; when it is ready let it cool in its own liquor; then take it out, and dish it, and serve it up cold, either whole or in slices.

Nowadays a boar's head is stuffed with ham, tongue, sausage meat and truffles and the ears, eyes and tongue removed, although the snout is allowed to remain. It is cooked for six hours and accompanied by a boar's head sauce, which is very similar to Cumberland sauce but contains horse-radish.

Parcel-gilt standing cup, the cover embossed and chased with royal arms of Charles II 1676. Latin inscription recording its gift to the Barber-Surgeons Company in 1676 by Charles II. (P.105.)

Vintners' wager cup dating around 1680. It is in the form of a milkmaid, dressed in the style of the mid-seventeenth century. Her petticoat forms the cup and above her head she holds a smaller cup embossed with foliage.

The feast of the boar's head is a modern revival of an old pagan tradition, practised by the Vikings. The boar, apart from being wild and ferocious, was also a Royal Beast. A truly conscientious host, wishing to honour his guest with a dish that was a rare delicacy, would go out into the forest and, regardless of his personal safety, slay the noble beast, have it elaborately cooked and present it to his visitor as a culinary and sporting tour de force. Those who today receive invitations to this feast at the Cutlers, Armourers or Carpenters should therefore be mindful of the compliment they are being paid.

The Dyers and Vintners Companies have dinners for a Royal Bird–the swan. These two Companies are unique in that only they are allowed the Mark and Game of Swans on the River Thames. It is one of those quaint anachronisms for which there is no documentary explanation. Nobody quite knows why and when the Vintners and the Dyers were allowed to share the sovereign's monopoly of these Royal Birds, but certainly the Vintners owned swans from the beginning of their first records.

In the fifteenth century swan was a luxury which only the rich could afford to serve in any quantity at their banquets. The Brewers Company were one of the most gastronomically ambitious guilds. At their feast in 1425 they spent £8 on poultry alone–including twenty-one swans at 3s. 9d. each. The geese at 8d, capons at 6d, partridges and woodcocks at 4d, were not nearly as expensive. The Brewers' sumptuous banquets irritated Richard Whittington when he was Lord Mayor so much that he severely harassed them over the high prices of their beer, reputedly because he was jealous of their extravagant entertaining.

Swan could be roasted like a goose or a turkey: 'stuffed with herbs and fat pork, sealed in a paste of flour and water and roasted for 2–3 hours until tender. The crust could then be broken and the bird finished in the oven or on a spit for about 20 minutes.' It does not in fact taste as delicious as it sounds. One of the main problems with a swan is that its legs and wings are very tough with all the powerful swimming it does, and therefore need far slower cooking than the rest of the bird. In spite of consultations to devise a magic recipe between the Vintners, Dyers and St John's College, Cambridge (who also have a swan feast), no one has yet managed to cook the swan well enough today for it to live up to its medieval reputation. So at the swan feasts in the autumn only a ceremonial portion of a cygnet is served.

In the Middle Ages the entertainment was the feast itself. People had to make their own amusements and their idea of fun could be a fight, a pageant or a feast. The most important days in a guild's calendar were the Lord Mayor's Day, and the Patron Saint's Day—on which a Company elected the new Master and Wardens. The usual procedure was a church, election, feast, and the Armourers for example in 1585

> went to Church at 2 of the clock at afternoon where they had a sermon and afterwards came home to the Hall with their wives where was a seemly banquet at which the new Master and Wardens were chosen in the presence of the whole livery, their wives and some other grave citizens—and afterwards a Boy arrived armed, with a Virgin following him leading a lamb, came in, with a drum and flute before the Dinner, and after marching twice about the Hall the tables all set, they marched to the high tables with a speech.

Many Companies still have their most important dinner on election day, when it is part of the tradition to crown the newly elected Master and Wardens with garlands. These are often velvet caps ornamented either with silver badges or elaborate embroidery. They are valued possessions. The Carpenters, for instance, perform the ceremony of crowning with a fine set of Masters' garlands that are over three hundred years old.

The ceremony takes place during dinner, and used to involve a great deal of promenading around the tables by the retiring Master and Wardens. Sometimes those poor gentlemen were so occupied with parading and transferring their garlands that they had little time to do justice to their share of the food. At election celebrations of the Drapers in 1522, the Master and Wardens were so busy with the crowning ceremony at dinner, that they had to catch up afterwards at a side table, where they had 'swannys puddings, one neck of mutton in pike broth, two shoulders of mutton roast, four conies, eight chickens, six pidgeons and cold meat, plenty, and so departed'.

The most elaborate crowning which still takes place today is the Skinners' ceremony of 'Cocks and Caps' which is performed at their election dinner. The Skinners' peculiarity is that they try a cap on the heads of several guests until it is found to fit only the head of the newly elected Master, rather like Cinderella's slipper; then the same test is applied to the Wardens. The ceremony is further embellished by five silver-gilt cups, in the shape of cockerels, which are used for drinking to the new officers. The cups are a gift to the Company from Mr William Cockayne, Citizen and Skinner, who left money in his will in 1598 to provide 'five fair cups of the value of six score and ten pounds of good and lawful money of England of the form and fashion of a cock'. The ceremony occurs after the loving cup is

Skinners' silver-gilt loving cups, dated 1605 have a London hallmark, but they are thought to be Augsburg work. These are part of a set of five made for the Company from money bequeathed for the purpose by Mr. William Cockayne (elected Master in 1582 though he declined office).

finished, when the Clerk and ten junior liverymen leave the hall to don their gowns, and line up outside with five liverymen carrying the cocks and the other five carrying the caps. Led by a band, the Beadle and Clerk enter in dignified procession. With music playing they parade one and a half times round the hall, with a roll on the drum a cap is handed to the retiring Master—who by trial and error finds its rightful wearer—and with trumpet sound the Master drinks from one of Cockayne's cups a toast to the Master Elect. The procedure is repeated four more times, with music, trumpet and drum and further solemn circuits of the hall.

There might be a danger that with so much colourful ritual the importance of what was actually consumed would be overlooked. However, the Livery Companies pay as much attention to what they eat as to how they eat it. Few Companies entertain enough to justify keeping a large staff in the kitchen; some of them have a Beadle married to a good cook who is able to cope with court dinners and small lunches; but most need to call in an outside caterer for parties numbering over a hundred.

Ring and Brymer, the caterers who do eighty-five per cent of the cooking for livery dinners, were founded in 1690 and so they have a deep-rooted understanding of their very traditional business. Little that is frozen, other than ice cream, finds its way to the table. Meat is not permitted to become dry and tasteless from pre-cooking or pre-carving; roast beef, for instance, is best Scottish Aberdeen Angus cooked to the pink of perfection on the premises and carved during the dinner—it takes eight carvers to keep up with a party of three hundred.

A few years ago Ring and Brymer pioneered 'The City of London Feast'—a sort of parody of a livery banquet for the tourists. As real-life situations have to be exaggerated to make drama work on the stage, so the City Feasts served up to the tourists are Ring and Brymer's interpretation of what the visitors expect, rather than a detailed imitation of the real thing. The rosewater dishes, loving cups and snuff boxes are but part of the entertainment, which includes a lecture from a Beadle on the history of the guilds and practically everything typically English a foreigner might look for, from the roast beef of Old England to Morris dancers and the band of the Coldstream Guards. The feasts are held at halls such as the Painter Stainers, Fanmakers, Bakers or Watermen's, hired for the occasion. So successful have they turned out to be that the Connaught Rooms have followed Ring and Brymer's lead. They give their banqueting suite a bit of baronial colour with a few suits of armour, some standards and heraldic shields, then two or three nights a week from May to September do City Feasts for any number from fifty to a thousand. Entertainment includes Elizabethan musicians and dancing to a modern band as well as all the traditional livery trappings.

The popularity of ancient feasts and Elizabethan banquets would not be so great if the food were more genuinely medieval. For the fact is that what was actually eaten in the Middle Ages would be considered quite disgusting today. Only the hardiest cattle, pigs and sheep could survive the cold and scarcity of food in winter, so great numbers of weaker beasts had to be slaughtered in the autumn. Their carcasses were then strongly salted to preserve them for the ensuing months. In summer fresh meat was often very high. Consequently, the strong taste of the meat had to be disguised with spices, herbs and wine. A cook did not really feel satisfied unless by his art he could totally eradicate all trace of the original ingredients. His aim was to combine as much irreconcilable material in one dish as he could without making it impossible to eat. Before the introduction of forks in James I's reign the only utensils were a knife and spoon, and food tended to be served in small soggy pieces. Very few vegetables other than onions and garlic were eaten and fresh fruit was not as common as dried fruit such as raisins and dates.

The kitchen was a place of tremendous activity. In the middle of the stone floor would be great trestle tables with massive oak tops for working surfaces. On the walls hung copper pots and pans, ladles, strainers, graters, skimmers, knives and great flesh-hooks for scooping out the huge sides of pork and beef which were simmering in the cauldrons of boiling water over the open fires. The most indispensable gadget was the mortar and pestle, for grinding, braying and reducing ingredients to powder. The Merchant Taylors still have one of these in their kitchen though its usefulness has been superseded by more modern electric equipment.

Methods may have been primitive and the food unpalatable, nevertheless great care was taken in the preparation of dishes and their presentation could outshine many cordon bleu cooks of today. Roasted peacocks and pheasants came to the table dressed up again in all their feathers and this recipe from the Salters Company shows how a game pie was cooked and presented in the fourteenth century:

> For to make a most choice paste of game to be eaten at the feast of Christmas (17th Richard II, AD 1394)
> Take pheasant, hare and chicken, or capon of each one; with 2 partridges 2 pigeons and 2 conies, and smite them on pieces, and pick clean away therefrom all the bones that you may and therewith do them into a Foil (shield or crust) of good paste, made craftily in the likeness of a bird's body, with the livers and hearts, 2 kidneys of sheep, and forced meat and eggs made into balls. Cast thereto powder of pepper, salt, spice, vinegar, and pickled mushrooms; and then take the bones and let them seeth in a pot to make a good broth therefrom, and do it into the foil of paste, and close it up fast and bake it well and so serve it forth, with the head of one of the birds stuck at the one end of the foil and a great tail at the other and divers of his long feathers set in cunningly all about him.

The high quality of the guild dinners in the fourteenth century attracted the nobility of church and state and even royalty. In 1380 the Goldsmiths Company entertained the Lady Isabel, daughter of the King, Lord Latimer and other dignitaries 'which put the Wardens to great cost'. It is the Vintners, however, who according to legend outclassed all the others by entertaining five crowned heads at one time. Unfortunately the Company has no record of this royal flush of visitors, but the legend is substantiated by Stow. The tradition has been preserved for over six centuries in the Company's toast: 'The Vintners Company may it flourish root and branch for ever with Five and the Master'.

In the fifteenth and sixteenth centuries the guilds' entertaining increased in scale and magnificence. Members brought not only their wives but their families and servants too. The floor of the vast common hall where the feast took place might be strewn with flowers and on the tables would be gold and silver vessels. The most splendid object was the salt; a magnificent piece of plate which was a medieval device for separating the sheep from the goats. The Masters, Wardens and distinguished guests sat above the salt and the more ordinary members of the Company sat further down the table below it. Sometimes a distinction was also made in what they were given to eat. For instance, at the Drapers' feast in 1516, the top table and the ladies in their separate rooms were served with 'brawn and mustard, capon boiled, swan roasted, pike, venison baked and roast; jellies, pastry, quails, sturgeon, salmon, wafers and hippocras. For the livery below the salt, four sirloins of beef "cut through the ox", six sheep and a calf.' When the dinner was finished the children and servants who were left outside in the courtyard were allowed in to finish the leftovers.

Gilt salt-cellar dated 1698, which was given to the Upholders in 1832 by Sir William Rawlins. At each corner stands a pavilion, which is the device of the Company.

The vast quantities of food provided by the Company were not always all eaten on the spot and many of the poorer members used to come away with enough leftovers to keep their households in food for a week. As time went on this practice caused many severe notices in the minutes of the Companies. The Coachmakers and Coach Harness Makers in the seventeenth century stipulated that 'no Master shall give unto his own or any other servant any meat from off the table on the penalty of 10 shillings'. Also that 'no liveryman shall bring any person save his wife on like penalty of 10 shillings'. About the same time other Companies had similar rules with varying fines for disobedience. The Armourers Company said:

> It is now here ordered and agreed by this Court that hereafter no Master, Warden, Assistant or Liveryman of the Company or their wives at any dinner or feast kept in this Hall shall presume to cut any meat or provisions and send it from the table to be sent to their houses or conveyed out of this Hall upon pain of forfeit 6s. 8d. for every time he or she shall do contrary to this order.

Consequently Companies developed very strict rules that food once it had been taken into the hall was not allowed out again. So if a new dish had to be started to give one liveryman a second helping the whole dish must be left in the room and not taken back to the kitchen. At the end of the dinner all that was left in the room was 'disposed of by the Beadle'. This practice continued in some Companies until the Second World War.

But back in the fifteenth century part of the leftovers were the guests' plates. These were trenchers, a sort of plate made of coarse bread, which sometimes when well saturated with sauce were eaten by the absent-minded. Otherwise the trenchers were swept into a basket at the end of a meal and given to the poor. Food was set upon the table in dishes like modern hors d'oeuvres and in each course there would be a variety of game, meat and delicious little pastry side dishes. Guests would be grouped in messes—eight to ten to each mess—and would help themselves to the various dishes on the table before them. An election dinner of the Brewers Company in Henry v's reign illustrates how each course was a meal in itself, yet people were not expected to eat every dish in the course:

> First course—Brawn with mustard; cabbages to the potage; swan standard; capons roasted; great custards. Second course—Venison in broth, with white mottrews, cony standard; partridges with cocks roasted; leche lumbard, doucettes with little parneaux. Third course—Pears in syrup; great birds with little ones together; fritters, payn puff with a cold bake meat.

To drink there were '22 gallons of strong ale, 18 gallons of

"penny" or medium ale, 36 gallons of light ale'. Leche lumbard was either 'A kind of jelly, made of cream, isinglas, sugar and almonds with other compounds' or 'pork pounded in a mortar with eggs, raisins, dates, sugar, salt, pepper, spices, milk of almonds and red wine, the whole boiled in a bladder'.

Feasts got off to very complicated starts. At first there would be much ceremonial washing—necessitated by the fact that the guests would eat from a common dish with their fingers. Then with a good deal of trumpeting a procession of servants would parade around the hall bearing the steaming dishes of the first course. Throughout the meal musicians would play and there would be a minstrel with his harp to tell wonderful tales in verse. As time went on and party-giving became more polished

Parcel-gilt tazza 1532. A rare example of domestic plate in the early Renaissance style of the first half of the sixteenth century, it was given to Arlington church in the nineteenth century for use as an almsdish. The Goldsmiths Company bought it in 1953 to prevent it leaving the country.

a host expected his chef to produce mysterious pies and table decorations to ensure that the banquet started on the right note of hilarity. Instructions from the *Cooks and Confectioners Dictionary*, 1724, gives details of how 'Some ancient Artists in Cookery inform us, that in former Days, when good House-keeping was in Fashion among the English Nobility, they used to begin or conclude their Entertainments, and divert their Guests with pretty Devices'. These were carefully contrived castles and ships, which had cannon that fired real gun-powder and eggshells filled with rosewater. The central attraction might be a pair of pies, one containing live frogs and the other live birds.

> These being prepared and placed in Order on the Table. First of all, one of the Ladies is persuaded to draw the Arrow out of the Body of the Stag, which being done, the Claret-wine issues out like Blood out of a Wound, and causes some small Admiration in the Spectators; which being over, after a little Pause, all the Guns on one Side of the Castle are by the Train, discharged against the Ship, and afterwards the Guns of one Side of the Ship against the Castle . . . as if in a Battle. This causing a great Stink of Powder, the Ladies or Gentlemen take up the Egg-shells of perfumed Water, and throw them at one another. This pleasant Disorder being pretty well laughed over, and the two great Pies still remaining untouched, some or other will have the Curiosity to see what's in them, and liting off the Lid of one pie out jump the Frogs; this makes the Ladies skip and scamper, and lifting up the Lid of the other, out fly the Birds, which will naturally fly at the Light, and so put out the Candles, and so with leaping of the Frogs below, and flying of the Birds above, it will cause a surprising and diverting Hurly-Burly amongst the Guests in the Dark; after which, the Candles being lighted, the Banquet is brought in, the Musick sounds, and the Particulars of each Person's Surprize and Adventures furnish Matter for diverting Discourse.

In 1607 the Merchant Taylors Company spent over £1000 on entertaining King James I and his son Prince Henry at their election feast. On the King's arrival 'a very proper child well spoken, being clothed like an angel of gladness with a paper of frankincense burning in his hand, delivered a short speech containing eighteen verses, devised by Ben Jonson the poet, which pleased his Majesty marvellously well' Tremendous trouble had been taken to provide enough music. Suspended about the hall was a ship floating between heaven and earth and carrying singers dressed in silk seamen's costume. On the other side of the hall in musicians' galleries were seven lute-players. Loud music from the hall itself almost overwhelmed the efforts of the performers suspended above the seething throng. The King and Queen dined privately in the King's Chamber, where there had been placed a 'very rich pair of organs, whereupon Mr John Bull, Doctor of Music and a brother of this Company, did play during all the dinner-time'. A window had been made in the King's Chamber for the King and Queen to watch the antics below and when

> the Master and Wardens went with garlands on their heads to publish the election, the Prince was graciously pleased to call for the Master's garland and put it on his own head, whereat the King who was watching through the window did very heartily laugh. After all which, his Majesty came down in the Great Hall, and sitting in the Chair of State did hear a melodious song of farewell sung by three men in the ship, which song so pleased his Majesty that he caused the same to be sung three times over.

All this expenditure on royal entertainment was not entirely wasted, since by their extravagant hospitality a Company might attract members from outside its trade whose wealth and rank would bring added prestige and power to its name. On the occasion described above when Prince Henry had been presented with a purse of fifty pounds by the Master he said he would not only himself be free of the Company, 'but required all the lords present that loved him and were not free of other companies to follow his example, whereupon three ambassadors, eighteen nobles, and some seventy gentlemen signified their willingness to do so'.

The £1000 the Merchant Taylors spent on their feast at the turn of the century was a tremendous sum in those days, especially when compared to what other Companies were spending. The Salters Company had been able to feed fifty people for a paltry £1 13s. 11½d. in 1506, a century earlier. Their bill of fare was:

36 Chickens	4s. 5d.	Herbs	1s. 0d.
1 swan & 4 geese	7s. 0d.	2 dishes of butter	4d.
9 rabbits	1s. 4d.	4 breast of veal	1s. 5d.
2 rumps of beef tails	2d.	bacon	6d.
6 quails	1s. 6d.	quarter load of coals	4d.
2 oz pepper	2d.	faggots	2d.
2 oz cloves & mace	4d.	3 gallons Gascon wine	2s. 4d.
1½ oz saffron	6d.	1 bottle Muscovadine	8d.
3 lbs sugar	8d.	cherries & tarts	8d.
2 lbs raisins	4d.	salt	1d.
1 lb dates	4d.	verjuice and vinegar	2d.
1½ lbs comfits	2d.	paid the cook	3s. 4d.
1½ hundred eggs	2½d.	perfume	2d.
4 gallons curds	4d.	1½ bushels of meal	8d.
1 doz. gooseberries	2d.	water	3d.
bread	1s. 0d.	garnishing the vessels	3d.
1 kilderkin of ale	2s. 3d.		

£1 13s. 11½d.

Compared with this the Brewers' dinner in 1425, when they had those twenty-one expensive swans, is high at £38. The Dinner Book of the Drapers Company gives details of an election feast of 1564, when the celebrations went on for three days. The bill for eighty-nine guests came to £82 9s. 4d., just under £1 a head. This included food, wine, servants, fuel, entertainment: 'Musician and his whole noise 13/4d', and extras such as perfumery and flowers. Allowing for the different dates, there is still an enormous variety in the scale of hospitality indulged in by different Companies, even in those early days.

One of the most costly items on the bills of fare was meat and game, for many centuries the mainstay of the citizens' diet. To reduce the demand for meat the Church imposed fast days which were as important for economic as for religious reasons. The Church's ban on meat on so many days of the year encouraged the eating of 'that abundance of fish which the sea yieldeth' and made it possible for a number of cattle to be conserved. A typical proclamation dated 1595 points out that 135,000 head of beef 'might be spared a year, in the City of London, by one day's abstinence in a week'.

By the seventeenth century forks had made their appearance and roast meats, tarts and pies were therefore easier to eat. Food became less sloppy; with British marine supremacy it also became more imaginative; people benefited from greater imports of commodities like sugar which meant there were more delicious sweetmeats included in the bills of fare. Smoking was highly fashionable at Court and tobacco and clay pipes were provided at table as part of the entertainment. This rise in the standard of living is reflected in the Weavers' election day feast in 1672, which though it cost £66, was more luxurious than that of the Salters a century and a half earlier:
Pullets and bacon
2 venison per upper table
1 venison per each of other tables
roast turkey
umble pie
roast beef–a piece to each table
roast capon
custard
tart
fruit, 2 dishes to each mess

Umble pie was a cheap dish made of offal, rather like a haggis, and it is from this that we get the expression 'to eat (h)umble pie'. In 1674 it was made thus:

> Boil your meat reasonable tender, take the flesh from the
> bone, and mince it small with beef-suet and marrow, with the

This picture which hangs on the staircase in Vintners Hall is a copy of the one by Chevalier Tayler in the old Royal Exchange. It depicts the famous occasion in the fourteenth century when the Vintners at an extravagant feast given by Sir Henry Picard, entertained no less than five kings.

Sir Henry Picard: Master of the Vintners Company: entertaining the Kings of England, France, Scotland, Denmark and Cyprus ✦ Painted by A. Chevallier Tayler:

liver, lights and heart, a few sweet herbs and currants, season it with netmeg pepper and salt, bake it in the form of an umble pie and your palate shall hardly distinguish which is which.

By the eighteenth century the order of dishes had become more pronounced: for the first course there would be two alternative turtle soups, one thick, one clear, and a wet and a dry fish. Cod was eaten a great deal until 1820 and there was usually a fried fish of some sort. For the second course there would be meat and poultry and for the third sweet and game. Left on the table at the end of the meal would be a variety of cakes, ices, sweetmeats and fruit.

Carving was one of the accomplishments of a gentleman and guests would carve for themselves or their neighbours in each mess. A complicated vocabulary was needed to ask for some meat: 'wing me a partridge' they would have said, or 'allay me a pheasant'. For each animal there was a different term for carving it: disfigure a peacock, dismember a heron, truss a chicken, spoil a hen, sauce a capon, lift a swan, break a deer, thigh a pigeon, rear that goose, barb a lobster or tame a crab. So dinner could contain social hazards for the Lord Mayors and Aldermen, many of whom were men who had started from the bottom rung and reached the top of their ladder either by hard and assiduous trading, or by judicious marriage.

In spite of these refinements City feasts in the eighteenth century were not noted for their decorum. Although those above the salt might be eating their dinner with all the hesitation of good manners, those below it were more inclined to fall upon their food and drink with impatient appetites. Poor William Hickey, attending the banquet for the incoming Lord Mayor, Sir Watkin Lewis, in November 1780, could hardly do full justice to his turtle, venison pies and grapes for the hurly burly around him:

> In the body of the hall in five minutes after the guests took their stations at the tables the dishes were entirely cleared of their contents, twenty hands seizing the same joint or bird and literally tearing it to pieces. A more determined scramble could not be, the roaring noise was deafening and hideous which increased as the liquor operated, bottles and glasses flying across from side to side without intermission. Such a bear garden I never beheld. This abominable and disgusting scene continued till near 10 o'clock when the Lord Mayor, Sheriffs and nobility adjourned to the ball and card rooms and the dancing commenced. Here the heat was in no way inferior to that of the hall and the crowd so great there was scarce a possibility of moving.

Sometimes the confusion was increased by the pressure of uninvited guests. One of the old pensioners living in a Weavers Company almshouse caused such a commotion by gatecrashing the Weavers' St James's Day feast in 1746 and 'by his behaviour gave great offence to diverse of the Liverymen' that Beadles were subsequently instructed that if any pensioner attempted to dine at 'Public Entertainments' he was 'to be removed accordingly'.

The Coopers Company in 1704 attributed the lack of decorum at their dinners to the presence of the women at their feasts and ungallantly resolved,

> whereas for several years past it has been usual to invite the several wives of the Assistants and Livery of this Company to dine at the Hall annually upon the Lord Mayor's Day, the Court now taking notice of the clamorous confusion and great disorders that of late years have thereby happened, have though fit and ordered that for time to come no woman whatsoever shall be invited to dine on that day, nor be admitted into the Hall upon any account whatsoever.

A design for a scene from 'Chrysalaneia', the pageant performed on Lord Mayor's Day 1616, devised by Anthony Munday for the Fishmongers Company. In honour of the special amity between the Goldsmiths and Fishmongers Companies, Munday included the Goldsmiths' leopard, mounted by the King of the Moors, 'hurling gold and silver every way about him' (see page 143).

It seems a bit hard on the poor ladies to blame them for disgraceful behaviour when really all the Company were doing was looking for an excuse to save money on their dinners by cutting down the numbers. About this time Companies like the Coopers were having difficulty in financing their dinners. Originally the cost of Company hospitality was borne by those attending, as specified in the Grocers' Ordinances of 1348, 'every member having a wife or companion should bring her to dinner or a lady in her place should she be ill, or being great with child and just near her delivery, without any other exception and pay 5 shillings'. Payment of food, wine or even provision of the whole dinner was sometimes meted out as a punishment. In 1382 Alderman John Sely of Walbrook, who appeared in a cloak without a lining at the Church of St Peter Cornhill at the feast of Pentecost, as a punishment had to entertain the Mayor and Corporation to dinner at his house on the Thursday following. But by the fifteenth and sixteenth centuries the leaders of the guilds were rich men who could afford to pay for dinner for all the Company, and so the cost of the annual feast was met by the Stewards and Wardens. This meant that in later years when Companies like the Coopers were declining with the loss of trade control, they found it difficult to find men of sufficient means to undertake the task of Steward. Anyone refusing to serve in 1643 was fined £20, but a plea of poverty was taken into consideration. In hard times the dinners were dropped altogether even by some of the Great Twelve. At the end of the eighteenth century the Girdlers Company had a particularly difficult time finding members to serve as Stewards. In 1759, for instance, two Girdlers were excused on signing an affidavit that they did not possess property worth more than £120.

But in the nineteenth century those Companies with large resources were paying for dinners out of their corporate funds and they were getting down to serious eating. As their character had slowly altered from craft guild to select club, the women were dropped from the guest list and dancing from the agenda. Banquets were a model of Victorian propriety. One of William Hickey's successors dining at the Ironmongers Company in 1875 describes a 'goodly banquet and pleasant music, well-chosen songs and duets and appropriate toasts'. He recalls dipping into the 'famous rosewater dish and washing one's face at the dinner table'. The chairs were in fact so widely spaced and there was such a quantity of food on the table that dinners tended to be eaten in silence which induced a slightly melancholy air to the traditionally festive occasions. By this time the carving was being done at the side of the room by servants. Large displays of dishes at each course for people to choose from became impracticable and the number of courses

Leathersellers' standing cup and cover in silver set with amethysts, designed by C. R. Ashby in 1899. It was presented to the Company by Colonel S. N. Bevington, Master 1897 to 1898.

lengthened and the choice of dishes in each course was shortened to two.

The dish most popular with Livery Companies was turtle soup and the frequency with which it appeared at their tables in the nineteenth century came under attack from the Liberals as part of their general disapproval of Company feasting. A pamphlet entitled *The Curse of Turtledom* roundly abused them for their decimation of the turtle population and some lively articles in the *Spectator* followed. Turtles were discovered in the Americas during the forays of Raleigh and Drake. Unlike most edible delicacies they travelled well, as they could be kept alive in a little water in the ship's hold, but although they were one of the few exotic imports from the new world capable of surviving the journey, they were too tough to eat on arrival in this country. However, they did make the most delectable soup, which became popular at banquets partly for its delicious flavour and partly for its effective pre-digestive qualities.

Left to nature only 2 per cent of turtle eggs hatch successfully The mother turtle lays her eggs on the open beach and then abandons them to be hatched in the heat of the sun. From then on they are the prey of every predatory creature around the water's edge. Even after hatching the baby turtles can be gobbled up by hungry gulls, while hurrying over the hundred yards of beach to the sea. Turtle 'growers' collect the eggs from the beaches and hatch them in secure turtle farms where eighty per cent survive, five per cent of which are returned to the beaches to lay more eggs for the next generation. Thus the demand in the kitchen has in fact benefited the turtle population. This argument does not, however, convince the conservationists of this century, who continue to campaign against the eating of turtles in soup. An enterprising American company has therefore started breeding these creatures on the Cayman Islands, to ensure that the City dinners will not lack one of the most traditional of first courses.

All livery feasting stopped during the First World War, and by that time dinners had many courses with no alternatives. A normal livery dinner would be like the one held by the Turners Company in 1913 which had nine courses plus dessert and coffee, with a choice of seven different wines, and liqueurs; six toasts were drunk entailing eight speeches. The musical entertainment after dinner was provided by five solo artists, and the words printed in full on the elaborate booklet containing menu, toast list and table plan.

Between the wars the dinners were if anything even longer and it was possible to face as many as twelve courses, plus accompanying wines and speeches, which demanded a strong constitution of those frequently attending City functions. All feasting ceased again during the Second World War and by the time the Companies were able to stretch their culinary imagination again, the years of rationing had so conditioned the minds and contracted the stomachs of post-war liverymen that dinners of the past seemed excessive. A normal City dinner today therefore would only be four or five courses.

It is probably only the Great Twelve and a few of the more affluent Minor Companies who can still afford to give their liverymen free dinners. Though Stewards and Wardens no longer bear these expenses, in Companies like the Cutlers they do pay a token £10.50 and are reminded, in their letter of appointment, of the days when it was part of the burden of their office to foot the bill for dinner for all. The majority of Companies now ask their members to make full payment towards any functions they attend.

One or two Companies, such as the Spectacle Makers, the Cutlers and the Turners, have been fortunate in having among their members in the past a benefactor who left money to be used to augment the Company's hospitality. In the case of the Spectacle Makers it was a small amount left to them in the reign of Queen Anne and the entire income from the bequest now goes to relief of members and their families. But the Cutlers inherited from Captain Boot in 1901 £40,000 to be spent on an annual banquet on his birthday at which food and wine should be of the best. This munificence was copied by Richard Gardner Williams, who left to the Turners Company a similar sum 'to provide the cost of an Annual Dinner to all Members of the Company on the 24th day of February in each year'. Every year therefore on the birthday of their benefactor the members of the Turners Company meet at Apothecaries Hall for the Gardner Williams Commemoration Dinner. Such a dinner might be as follows: consommé royale with dry Madeira; scampi Newburg washed down by Corton Charlemagne 1964, saddle of lamb, button sprouts and duchesse potatoes, accompanied by Chateau Lafite Rothschild 1956, a raspberry sorbet enhanced by a glass of Chateau Climens 1966, canape epicure capped with a glass of Offley 1956, coffee and liqueurs; music from the Scholars, a group of former choral scholars of King's College, Cambridge. The evening is brought to a fitting close by the traditional Clerk's toast, 'To the pretty maids, the merry wives and the buxom widows of the Turners of London'.

Livery dinners today may not be as hilarious as they were in the seventeenth and eighteenth centuries, nor as lengthy as in the Middle Ages; and certainly not such a gastronomic endurance test as they were a hundred years ago, yet their standard of entertainment is as high as any in London. The food is of the best, only equalled by the wine, and this combination, served with ceremonial, accompanied by music, dramatically lit by sparkling chandeliers or a hundred candles, and adorned with priceless silver, creates a sense of secure well-being equal to anything achieved in the past.

Chapter 5

Processions

And pomp, and feast, and revelry
With mask, and antique pageantry
Such sights as youthful poets dream
On summer eves by haunted streams.

from *L'Allegro*, by JOHN MILTON

Precedence is to a guild what the league table is to a football club, and the Great Twelve are in the first division. Long ago they played the major part in civic affairs and the Lord Mayor was elected exclusively from among their ranks. So much so that if he were not a member of a Company belonging to one of the Great Twelve, then he had to join one. This tradition lasted until 1742, when Robert Willimott, an independently minded Cooper, refused to transfer and thus became the first Lord Mayor from a Minor Company. Nowadays the situation is reversed and it is the Minor Companies which play the most active part in civic politics. Out of twenty-nine Lord Mayors since the war, only eleven have been from a Major Company. Nevertheless, in stature, wealth and influence the Great Twelve still lead the way, and whither they go the rest feel bound to follow.

Precedence was achieved in a mysterious way and the right of one guild to precede another is not determined by any obviously clear-cut criteria. Age does not seem to have been important—the Weavers, with the oldest charter, are forty-second and the Saddlers twenty-fifth; nor size—the Shipwrights and Stationers Companies are bigger than many of those who precede them. Wealth was undoubtedly a contributing factor, since the London subsidy roll shows that in 1319 the wealthiest class of taxpayers were drapers, mercers, pepperers, fishmongers, woolmongers, skinners and goldsmiths. All these, with the exception of the woolmongers, were crafts whose guilds were among the top twelve Companies. Yet the Leathersellers (fifteenth), Carpenters (twenty-sixth) and Brewers (fourteenth) were almost as wealthy as some of those above them in the league, so riches alone were not enough. It was political power which also helped to establish some of the leading guilds, which in the thirteenth and fourteenth centuries followed the principle that God helps them who help themselves and established their positions by force majeure.

Confrontation between status conscious guilds varied from scuffles between contentious apprentices, with the damage limited to a broken head or two, to battles between armed men which had more serious consequences. In 1226, for instance, a number of armed men from the Goldsmiths and Merchant Taylors Companies fought a pitched battle on an appointed night, as a result of which many were killed or wounded. The mêlée was broken up by the City Sheriffs, who executed thirteen of the ringleaders. In 1340 a similar battle took place between the Fishmongers and the Skinners, which was vigorously repressed by Andrew Aubrey, a decisive Grocer Lord Mayor. Although two fishmongers were executed for their part in this affair, the Company nevertheless managed to hold on to their position of fourth in the order of precedence. It was a position they had also to defend from the Goldsmiths, who came fifth; the Skinners were left to dispute the sixth place with the Merchant Taylors. Their rivalry continued to provoke acrimonious quarrels up to 1484, when the Lord Mayor decreed that they should take it in turns to be sixth and seventh and his Solomon-like decision brought their dispute to an end. The practice is still in force and each year the Skinners and Merchant Taylors alternate between sixth and seventh place, bringing a special amity to the Companies and giving rise to the expression 'all at sixes and sevens'.

A curious result of past quarrels is that those Companies who fought so violently with each other for supremacy in the past now have particularly strong ties of friendship. The Goldsmiths and Fishmongers, as a result of their quarrel, have a very long-standing and special amity; for many centuries they wore a piece of each other's dress—the Fishmongers wearing hoods in the colour of the Goldsmiths' livery and the Goldsmiths hoods in the colour of the Fishmongers'.

Until Henry VIII's reign there was still a certain amount of variation among the Companies. The first twelve Companies named to attend Edward IV's Queen to her coronation in 1467 were the Mercers, Drapers, Grocers, Fishmongers, Goldsmiths, Vintners, Skinners, Taylors, Ironmongers, Salters, Haberdashers and Girdlers. A little later in the same reign the first twelve appointed to set a watch on the vigil of St Peter and St Paul included the Dyers. When Richard III came to the throne the Scriveners were among those Companies at the head of the procession that escorted him on his entry into the City of London. The position was finally regularized in 1515, when the

Lord Mayor and Aldermen drew up the list of precedence. The order of the Great Twelve has never altered since then, although there was some disagreement between the Shearmen (who later amalgamated with the Fullers to become the Cloth-workers) and the Dyers as to the twelfth place. In 1518 the Shearmen won, leaving the Dyers relegated to thirteenth place as head of the Minor Companies. Among the Minor Companies there has been a certain amount of chopping and changing due to amalgamation and the disappearance of several guilds. The list for them is the same now as in 1884, but the mystique surrounding the question of precedence has not lasted into modern times. Those seven Companies which have appeared in the twentieth century take their places at the bottom of the list in simple chronological order.

Precedence was valued for a place a guild was entitled to take in public processions, and it is still strictly adhered to on the rare occasions when the Livery Companies appear collectively in public. Processions, plays and pageants were an important part of a guild's life at one time, and there are some colourful traces left in their behaviour now which they have preserved as part of their medieval inheritance. The public appearances of some Livery Companies today, however, are not always in the most obvious places. The unsuspecting visitor to London, exploring the City one summer's day, could be taken completely unawares by a strange little procession of men, dressed in furred gowns and flat Tudor caps, carrying posies and preceded by a Beadle in the full glory of official insignia. They would be the Court of some Livery Company processing to church on the guild's patron saint's day. In the case of the Vintners there would also be porters in white aprons sweeping the streets with birch brooms. The birch brooms and the posies are a reminder of the days when the streets were so filthy that a way had to be swept through the debris, and herbs carried as a protection against the diseases borne on the fetid air. The English are peculiarly adept at performing such ceremonies without looking ridiculous or theatrical. They seem to have a special facility for carrying off the whole anachronistic performance in a most natural manner.

Formerly every Company used to process to church on their patron saint's day before the election of their new officers for the year, but now only a handful maintain this tradition: the Merchant Taylors on the feast of St John the Baptist in June, the Skinners on Corpus Christi, the Vintners, Saddlers, Iron-mongers and Carpenters on their respective saints' days in July, the Basketmakers and Painter Stainers in October. The rest of the Companies content themselves with putting in an appearance at the annual City and Guilds service at St Paul's in April. This is one of the three occasions during the year when

all the Livery Companies are assembled together in an impressive display of ancient guildry. Masters and Wardens wear their different coloured gowns; the Lord Mayor attends, arrayed in the sartorial trimmings of his office, accompanied by the Sheriffs, Aldermen and City Officers in the full splendour of their civic uniform.

The two other important ceremonies for the Livery Companies take place at Guildhall: these are the election of the Sheriffs on Midsummer's Day and the election of the Lord Mayor at Michelmas. The ceremony on Michelmas Day in the autumn, at which the new Lord Mayor is elected, may be something of a formality, but such is the combination of meaningful tradition and aweful pomp with which it is performed that the outcome appears the result of dignified deliberation. Before the election the Lord Mayor, Aldermen and City Officers, with appropriate piety, attend a short service in St Lawrence Jewry, a tradition instigated by Dick Whittington in the fifteenth century. On their return they find the Common Hall packed with liverymen anxious to exercise their ancient franchise. The procession that enters Guildhall carrying little posies is impressive. Twenty-five scarlet-robed Aldermen, each attended by his Ward Beadle, the Common Cryer in black gown and white wig carrying the official mace, the Sword Bearer in whose hand is the sword of state and on whose head is a heavy fur hat, another Beadle carrying another mace, two Chaplains, the City Marshal in plumed hat and military bearing and finally the reigning Lord Mayor, all walk slowly through the crowded hall to the hustings. This is a raised platform at the east end of the hall, the floor of which has been strewn with aromatic herbs. The herbs and the posies are still there to protect the civic dignitaries from the infectious air of the Middle Ages. For the actual voting the Lord Mayor and those Aldermen who 'have passed the Chair'—a Corporation expression for ex-Lord Mayors—leave the hall to remove any suspicion of personal influence. Then the Common Cryer calls on the liverymen to give him their attention. The names of some four or five Aldermen are read out, of which the liverymen elect two—one for the coming year and the other for the next year. The rest of the Aldermen then adjourn to the Aldermen's court room to vote for one of these two, and it is no surprise that they choose the one designated by the livery for the coming year. Once the full procession has returned to the hustings the Lord Mayor elect delivers a short speech expressing his willingness to serve. He is expected to give a short biographical account of himself and also to be somewhat overwhelmed—if he has any sense of history. Although for the past four years he has been preparing himself for his inevitable election, yet when he stands before the liverymen and contemplates the antiquity of the office to which he has just been elected, the moment is weighted with ghosts from the past. He may

One of the Vintners' wine porters with his birch broom resting on the steps of St. James Garlickhythe, having swept the street all the way from Vintners Hall for the Court of the Company.

The Wardens of the Vintners Company leaving the church of St. James Garlickhythe in procession, wearing their gowns and caps and carrying posies. This traditional progress to church takes place after the election of the Master on the Patron Saint's Day of the Company in July.

think of the men who have preceded him—men of great power, great humanity or even occasionally great wickedness—in whose footsteps he is about to follow.

After his election the new Lord Mayor conserves his energies for the year to come. He does not appear in public again until he goes to the House of Lords to receive from the Lord Chancellor the Queen's approval for his appointment. Then at the beginning of November his year of office begins on Lord Mayor's Day and he shows himself to the citizens of London in a spectacular street procession. The Lord Mayor's Show is divided into three different sections—civic, commercial and military. In the military section there are lots of bands and soldiers; in the commercial section, which takes the form of a pageant with a coherent theme, lots of elaborately decorated floats, and in the civic part the essential ingredients of a good procession, plenty of horses and carriages. The Lord Mayor's coach, four and a half tons of gilded and painted civic splendour, is drawn by six grey shire horses from the Whitbread stables and is escorted by a detachment of the Household Cavalry; with the Lord Mayor's bodyguard, pikemen and musketeers from the Honourable Artillery Company, walking alongside. The Livery Companies occupy about four carriages—one each for the mother Companies of the Lord Mayor and two Sheriffs; one for representatives of the Great Twelve, and every third year one for the Master and Wardens of the Pattenmakers. This, like so many Livery Company customs, stems from a clash of interest many centuries ago. The Pattenmakers used to have a march and dinner on the ninth of November every third year, and when the Lord Mayor's Day was moved from 29th October to 9th November with the reform of the calendar in 1752, the Pattenmakers' march through the City became entangled with that of the Lord Mayor's, sometimes with unfortunate results. So since the end of the eighteenth century the Pattenmakers have been persuaded to abandon their procession in return for a place in that of the Lord Mayor's.

On the second Saturday in November the various Livery Companies concerned assemble early in the morning at Guildhall, where they present their addresses to the Lord Mayor and Sheriffs before the start of the procession; then, refreshed with a glass of punch, they take their places in the carriages and at about half past eleven the show gets on the road. The route from Guildhall, past the Mansion House and to the Law Courts via Cheapside and Ludgate Hill, returning to the Mansion House via Victoria Embankment and Queen Victoria Street, covers a distance of two and a half miles with about half an hour allowed for the journey each way.

Four Beadle's staffheads cast in the arms of the respective companies: Merchant Taylors Company made by William Pitts and Joseph Preedy in 1795; Clothworkers Company made by Samuel Courtauld in 1755; Tallow Chandlers Company made in 1682; Parish Clerks Company 1787.

The overall organization of the Lord Mayor's Show is the responsibility of the City Remembrancer at Guildhall, but the details of the military part are normally co-ordinated by the Secretary of the City of London Territorial Auxiliary, and those of the pageant by a Pageant Master. Obviously plans for such an elaborate procession have to be inaugurated long before the Lord Mayor himself has been elected at the Guildhall in September. All correspondence about the arrangements before this time is therefore opened by a rather guarded phrase, 'in the event of the senior Alderman below the Chair being elected Lord Mayor he would wish . . .' and all details have to be finally approved by the Lord Mayor and Sheriffs' Committee when it first meets after his election. The expenses for the Lord Mayor's Show and Banquet on the Monday afterwards are met by the Lord Mayor and Sheriffs. In the case of the Show, the military expenses consist of feeding all the soldiers taking part; the pageants largely pay for themselves, as the firms entering floats do so at their own expense; and the Livery Companies are responsible for providing their own carriages.

It is the largest procession in the world which is carried out without any rehearsals, and it says a great deal for the efficiency of the organizers and the City police that it runs as smoothly as the daily changing of the guard at Buckingham Palace. There was once a minor disturbance when elephants in the procession ran amok. It was in 1930, when the Lord Mayor, the Rt. Hon. Sir W. Phene Neal, had chosen to include in his procession four elephants decorated with the trappings and caparisons of state processions in India. The animals, which had been hired from Mr Power's dancing elephants at Brixton, were accompanied by ten attendants, dressed in Indian processional costume. All went well until the procession passed a group of students from King's College who were waving a red lion mascot. The elephants, fooled by the lifelike resemblance of this mascot to their traditional enemy of the jungle, broke away from the line of route and made straight for the lion. The leading animal seized it with his trunk and dashed it to the ground, where it was trampled on by the others. The attendants then managed to regain control of their ponderous charges, which resumed the procession quietly as if nothing had happened. However, the panic among the tightly packed crowd when it imagined itself being charged by four rampaging ceremonial elephants caused a certain disorder which resulted in injury to some thirty spectators.

The elaborate progress of the Lord Mayor from Guildhall to the Law Courts is not just a public relations exercise by the Corporation of the City of London, designed to entertain the citizens and attract the tourists; it does have a legal purpose. The Lord Mayor has to be sworn in by the Lord Chief Justice and this is the reason for his conspicuous visit to the Law Courts. This simple constitutional necessity has been carried out by successive Lord Mayors for over seven and a half centuries. Before 1882 the justices used to sit at Westminster, and the Lord Mayor either went there or to the Tower to present himself to the Constable if the King or his justices were out of London. The first journeys were made on horseback and were modest ridings, with only minstrels and some of the Livery Companies accompanying the Lord Mayor.

This does not mean that in the thirteenth century processions were limited to a few minstrels on horseback. Indeed, the citizens' delight in pageantry was almost equal to their passion for feasting, both based on a desire for entertainment. But the most important festival of the year in those days was Midsummer's Eve. The pagan worship of Midsummer seems to have been observed all over Europe, and Christian communities invented their own reasons for celebrating it. In London the festivities took place during the setting up of the Watch for the ensuing year on the Vigil of St John, or Midsummer's Eve. The Watch—to which each guild contributed a certain number of men—consisted mainly of old soldiers and was the responsibility of one of the Aldermen in each of the City Wards. The guilds were also responsible for contributing to the lighting of the streets and they had to provide cressetts in allotted areas. These were large metal baskets which contained flaming materials and were carried on long poles. By the middle of the sixteenth century the setting of the Watch, which had been an excuse for a grand military muster, began to give way to the Lord Mayor's procession and more lavish display was concentrated on the civic scene.

Other opportunities for public celebration were the activities of royalty. Although they reigned with absolute power, rulers could still be flattered by demonstrations of favourable public opinion. So they encouraged the paraphernalia of pomp and pageantry with which the citizens indulged their royal entries, and at royal weddings, coronations and victory celebrations paraded through the city streets to see what had been devised in their honour.

The programme would consist of stationary pageants, moving processions or sometimes both. The pageants lined the royal route and dispensed music, flowers and allegorical compliments. Shakespeare mentions the citizens' warm reception of Anne Boleyn in *Henry VIII*:

2nd Gentleman: Tis well: the citizens
                I am sure, have shown at full their royal
                                minds—

KING CHARLES II.
triumphal Entry into the
City of London at his
Restoration.

> As, let 'em have their rights, they are ever
> forward
> In celebration of this day with shows,
> Pageants and sights of honour.

For Anne's coronation procession through the streets there were three main shows—one at Leadenhall, the second at the Standard in Cheap and the third at Little Conduit, also in Cheap, the main thoroughfare of the City. The plethora of pageants had so exhausted the pool of musical talent that the citizens had to ask Henry if they could borrow some of the royal minstrels to furnish their street theatres. Small displays at Fenchurch and Gracechurch paved the way for the big show at Leadenhall, 'where was built a sumptuous and costly pageant in manner of a castle'. In Cheap, the second pageant consisted of poems read by three graces—Hearty Gladness, Stable Honour and Continual Success—in praise of Anne, and the third contained a little play involving dramatic moments in the lives of various classical deities such as Juno, Pallas Athene, Venus and Mercury. All along the route lesser pageants dispensed music, speeches and a continual flow of red and white wine.

For the coronation celebrations of Richard II in 1377 the Goldsmiths erected a castle at the head of Cheap, which would do credit to a theatrical designer today: it had

> four towers, on each of which stood a beautiful virgin, who blew leaves of gold on the King, and threw counterfeit gold florins before him and his horse. Wine ran forth in abundance from two sides of this structure, which was surmounted by a gold angel; this stood between the towers and was so contrived that when the King came, it bowed down and offered him a crown.

Gifts, fountains flowing with wine, elaborate mechanical devices and pure and lovely maidens were important ingredients for a good royal tribute.

Moving processions also had their conventional figures, although they tended to concentrate more on the grotesque. Giants, puppets, Moors and wild men were some of the characters that used to delight the crowds. The legendary figures of Gog and Magog, two painted wooden replicas which are in the Guildhall, were two of the most popular giants. These twelve-foot monsters lumbering along in the processions could peer into the first floor windows of the houses lining the route, and pleasantly frighten the watchers on their beribboned balconies. The purpose of the green or wild men was to clear a way for the rest of the procession through the narrow streets. They were half-naked, desperate looking characters, with shaggy hair and beards, brandishing clubs or brooms. Other attendants were

A line engraving of King Charles II's triumphal entry into the City of London at his restoration. The City Companies spent a lavish £6,000 on the procession to escort him from the Tower to Whitehall before his coronation.

The celebrated fourteen-and-a-half foot high eighteenth-century figures of Gog and Magog which were made in 1708 by Captain Richard Saunders, an eminent carver in King Street. These colossal figures were a familiar feature in Guildhall until they were destroyed when the roof was burnt in December 1940. They were them replaced with nine foot figures made by David Evans. Gogmagog and Corineus, were mythical giants in the monkish chronicles of the Middle Ages, reputed to have fought on the side of the Trojans against the early inhabitants of Britain and it is from a popular shortening of these that the Guildhall giants came to be named.

men in armour and the Whifflers who, though dressed splendidly in velvet coats, also carried chains and staves, or swords, so that they could perform the dual task of clearing a way for the floats that followed and protecting them from the disorderly gangs who tended to appear as night fell.

The floats carried live actors, usually in the guise of allegorical or classical figures such as Arion sitting on a dolphin in a sea playing a harp. Some of these moving stages were wonderful works of art and those belonging to the Livery Companies were inspired pieces of mechanical ingenuity and costly ornamentation. Naturally such an expensive device was expected to survive more than one public airing and they were stored in the roof of a Company's hall and revamped from time to time. Some guilds had a special pageant chamber in which they stored the smaller props, and they put arsenic into the paste used to stick the figures together to 'save the giants from being eaten by the rats'. The Companies became known for their splendid floats; the Goldsmiths for their Castle, the Fishmongers for their Ship, but the most magnificent of all was the Mercers' Maiden Chariot. This was a piece of machinery twenty-two feet high, entirely covered with silver embossed work and drawn by nine white Flanders horses, three abreast, in rich trappings of silver and white feathers. The central figure on the chariot was a beautiful maiden dressed in pure white satin and crowned with a jewelled coronet. She was surrounded by over twenty superbly dressed allegorical figures representing all the virtues, and riding each of the horses were more allegorical characters.

Another feature in the processions and pageants staged by the guilds was trade symbolism. Animals were used a great deal in processions and the more rare and exotic the better. As most Companies had an animal for their sign these were used to advertise the guild's craft connections. The Goldsmiths' leopard, the Merchant Taylors' camel, the Cutlers' elephant, Clothworkers' ram and the Skinners' lynx added a bizarre touch to the already grotesque collection of performers in the cast. In the processions held for Edward I on his return from his victorious Scottish campaign the Fishmongers paraded no less than four gilt sturgeons, four salmon of silver and forty-eight knights on horses made to resemble water luces. The fur of wild animals being the trade of the Skinners, they were particularly given to using all sorts of beasts in their displays. A Skinner Lord Mayor in 1671 had a wilderness of every variety of shrub and tree inhabited by wild beasts, birds, two negro boys on panthers and a dancing bear; a few years later in another Skinner procession there were wolves, bears, panthers, leopards, sables and beavers together with dogs, cats, foxes and

Standing outside the hustings after the election of the Lord Mayor at Guildhall in 1973 are the outgoing Lord Mayor, Lord Mais, and the Lord Mayor elect, Sir Hugh Wontner, with the state trumpeters of the Household Cavalry.

Aldermen of the City of London with their Ward Beadles processing out of Guildhall after the election of the Lord Mayor.

Doggett Coat and Badge men wait outside Fishmongers Hall for the start of the annual Doggett's race. They are wearing their scarlet watermen's uniforms and silver badges, provided yearly under the Will of the late Mr. Thomas Doggett by the Fishmongers Company to the winner of the four-and-a-half-mile sculling race.

Swan Uppers from the Vintners Company searching for swans on the upper reaches of the Thames.

rabbits. The rabbits, the account says, were tossed up now and then into the balconies 'full oft upon the company's heads and being by them tost again into the crowd, afforded great diversion'. The chronicler does not relate whether the poor rabbits were alive, but judging by their ideas of diversion in the seventeenth century they probably were.

By this time pageants had become the work of experts. Although Shakespeare was too busy writing plays for the theatre, many of his contemporaries, such as Webster, and minor poets such as Middleton, Dekker and Mundy were writing pageants. Mundy was a particularly prolific pageant writer, and one of his greatest works was the spectacle he devised for the Fishmongers for the Lord Mayor's Show for Sir John Lemon in 1616. There were eight pageants consisting of the Fishmongers' ancient Ship, which had been appearing in processions for over three hundred years; Arion mounted on a dolphin; the King of the Moors mounted on a leopard hurling gold and silver coins to the crowds (the leopard was the symbol of the Goldsmiths Company and the inclusion of this pageant in the show was an example of the Fishmongers' special amity with the Goldsmiths); a large lemon tree to represent the Lord Mayor, with a pelican feeding her young with her own blood, symbolizing the Lord Mayor's self-sacrificing attitude to the citizens under his care; horsemen in armour with Wat Tyler's head on a spear; the Fishmongers' Pageant Chariot with Richard II surrounded by eleven royal virtues and drawn by a merman and a mermaid; the centre piece was 'a goodly bower—enclosing a fair tomb whereon in armour lyeth the imaginary body of Sir William Walworth'. On his approach the entombed hero of the Company rises and addresses the Lord Mayor:

And see my Lord this bower relates
How many famous magistrates
From the Fishmongers' ancient name
Successively to honour came.

The mermaid and merman looked very artistic but they lacked the physical strength to draw an elaborate pageant chariot any distance. Roads were bad enough inside the city walls, outside them they were mere country cart tracks beset with dangerous people and potholes. The brightly attired attendants could hardly be expected to manhandle the elaborate chariots through the mud and mire of country lanes, so for journeys outside the city walls the procession took to the water.

The river made a splendid thoroughfare for stately processions. Its banks were lined with the residential houses of nobles and prosperous merchants; gardens ran down to the water's edge, providing ideal vantage points from which to watch the specta-cle. The first Lord Mayor to go by barge was William Walderne in 1422, who, according to the records of the Brewers Company, was chosen Mayor on St Edmund's Day, 'when it was ordered that the aldermen and crafts should go to Westminster with him to take his charge, in barges, without minstrels'. But the man who recognized the river's full potential for dramatic display was Sir John Norman. For his Mayor's procession in 1453 he had a resplendent barge built at his own expense, which with its silver oars and other glittering accoutrements appeared to onlookers to burn on the water; in this vessel the flamboyant Draper set off in state, like a mayoral Cleopatra, to present himself to the justices sitting at Westminster.

The Livery Companies were quick to follow his lead. At first they hired their barges, decorating them with the Companies' insignia of shields, flags and banners. The Skinners borrowed the state barge of Cardinal Wolsey when they had a Lord Mayor in 1518. Churchmen seem to have been rich in barges, for in 1533 the Drapers, after Sir John Norman's splendid vessel had become unseaworthy, arranged to hire from the Archbishop of Canterbury 'his great barge, at such time as we shall have need to occupy it'. Their need was, however, subservient to that of the Archbishop for at the celebrations of Henry's fourth marriage, to Anne of Cleves, the archiepiscopal barge was already taking part and they had to hire a royal barge for the occasion.

However, by the seventeenth century most Companies had barges of their own. In the prow stood the Bargemaster, resplendent in his uniform, bearing on his sleeve a large silver badge with the Company's arms. Eighteen oarsmen manned the vessel, dressed in full skirted jackets laced with gold, breeches, stockings, buckled shoes and peaked velvet jockey caps. The passengers travelled aft of the oarsmen in the centre of the barge. One of the Apothecaries' barges had a curtained room like the cabin of a gondola for the passengers, which contained a raised seat for the Master, covered with crimson silk damask and a foot-rest. Other barges had covered platforms which accommodated people both inside and out. In the stern were the musicians, and the mate, who steered the vessel. Colourful banners streamed from prow and stern, and many a barge had the Company's patron saint as a figurehead. The stern transom was the highest part of these barges and therefore an ideal place for the arms of the Company, and some were richly embellished with intricate heraldic decoration. Even the rudder would be gaily painted with mermaids and sea creatures.

Brilliantly coloured and gilded replica of the Merchant Taylors' arms in carved wood which was once the tailpiece on their last barge, built in 1800. This 8 foot by 6 foot relic now hangs over the grand staircase in Merchant Taylors Hall.

The river was almost as crowded as the land during the City's welcome for Charles II's bride, Catherine of Braganza, in 1662. Early in the morning the barges of all the Livery Companies processed up river and lay at anchor in order of precedence. Then the Lord Mayor and Aldermen were rowed on to Chelsea where they met the King and Queen coming from Putney. Pepys complains that there were so many boats he could not see their Majesties: 'Anon came King and Queen in a barge under a canopy with 10,000 barges and boats, I think, for we could see no water for them, nor discern the King and Queen'. The Livery Companies had also staged elaborate floating pageants on the water. The Merchant Taylors contrived with considerable ingenuity to include not one but two camels in their pageant, which was a scene of a desert wilderness. 'A stage twelve foot by seven foot broad, arched with wild arbour, made in manner of a wilderness; the two camels are backed with two Indians. There are two Moors, that attend the camels as their guides. In the wilderness is seated an aged Man, representing a Pilgrim and attendants Faith, Hope and Charity'. As the Merchant Taylors' patron saint was St John the Baptist, they were always very fond of pageants depicting desert wildernesses containing naked men living off the fruit of the ground.

The organization of the Lord Mayor's procession was then the responsibility of his mother Company. It started at the Guildhall, and processed on land to the Tower, where the participants embarked. With the Lord Mayor's barge leading, followed by that of his mother Company, and all the rest in strict order of precedence, the flotilla rowed upstream to Westminster. The sound of drums, flutes and trumpets from the water-borne musicians floated upon the wind and mingled with the roar of the cannons firing from the wharves as the procession passed; the width of the river lent a distant enchantment to the gracefully gliding barges, which was more restful than the raucous excitement of junketings through the narrow streets. On the return journey the Companies disembarked at Blackfriars and returned to the Guildhall via St Paul's Churchyard. Here the richer guilds would have erected stands for their spectators, and the main pageants of the Show were then performed. Until 1711 the Lord Mayor covered the land part of the journey on horseback, but in 1710 Sir Gilbert Heathcote was ignominiously unseated from his animal on returning from Westminster and lest the dignity of succeeding Lord Mayors should be impaired by further equestrian disasters, a coach was built. A coach with four or six horses is an impressive vehicle and soon began to rival a barge as a means of transport. In 1756 the Lord Mayor's gilded coach, which is still used today, was built and the procession often then went the whole way to Westminster by land. The barges were still used for other formal occasions, such as Lord Nelson's funeral in 1806, when all the Livery

Companies who could get waterborne escorted the great admiral's coffin in its black draped barge from Greenwich to Whitehall. Throughout the century the Company barges were used for social outings, and fashionable Richmond, where the Regent kept his mistress Mrs Fitzherbert, was an ideal spot for an outing. The Stationers Company, for instance, had annual expeditions to the Star and Garter Hotel at Richmond, where they dined in a manner in keeping with the style of a Livery Company.

By the nineteenth century the river was not the sparkling clean and manoeuvrable thoroughfare it had once been. Its banks were lined with dirty warehouses and its surfaces congested with a greatly increased number of commercial sailing barges plying to and fro with cargoes from the great ships lying at anchor in the Port of London. Roads, however, were benefiting from the engineering genius of John McAdam and journeys by land became a more attractive prospect. So as the Company barges fell into disrepair they were not replaced, and when the Lord Mayor finally gave up his barge in 1858 the others followed suit. The story goes that half the livery barges were bought by Cambridge and the other half by Oxford to turn into college boathouses. The Cambridge ones were sunk at sea on their journey round the coast, which explains why for a time Oxford had many more unusual boathouses than Cambridge.

All that is left of these barges today are a few relics, some figure heads and one or two good models. The Goldsmiths, for instance, have the gilded seventeenth-century figure of St Dunstan from their second barge overlooking the main staircase in Goldsmiths Hall, and the Fishmongers, Clothworkers, Merchant Taylors and Stationers fine models of their last barges. The Ironmongers even have a snuff box made out of barge timbers. Nearly every Company that once had a barge points proudly to some relic displayed in a prominent place in their hall.

The disappearance of state barges has not utterly put an end to all Company river outings. There are two occasions during the year which bring out upon the water with their banners flying those Companies which have maintained a river connection. Although hired motor launches lack some of the panache of the former craft, the occasions themselves are marked with an ancient style and total irrelevance which makes them especially attractive. One is when the Court of the Vintners and Dyers Companies with their guests make a lunch-time expedition by river to watch their Swan Uppers at work. Each year these two Companies are responsible for the marking of a certain number of cygnets, as a result of their unique privilege of the Mark and Game of Swans on the River Thames. There are about a thousand swans on the Thames of which about 150 have two nicks on their beaks and belong to the Vintners, while about 140 with one nick belong to the Dyers. All unmarked swans at liberty belong to the Queen. The Queen's right to own swans, and thereby the ancient privilege of the Dyers and Vintners, was very nearly swept away by the Wild Creatures and Forest Laws Bill of 1971, which attempted to tidy up some of the more illogical feudal relics of the statute book. However, Her Majesty refused to allow the royal prerogative to be interfered with in this way, so the new Act includes a clause specifically safeguarding her rights in respect of swans. For a week in July a small search party of six rowing boats, containing the Bargemasters and swan herdsmen from the Queen, the Dyers and the Vintners, comb the reaches of the Thames from Westminster pier to Runnymede looking for cygnets. Needless to say this simple swan husbandry is accomplished with the maximum amount of colour and ancient tradition. The Bargemasters are dressed in an appropriate kind of semi-naval uniform with a swan's feather in the cap, and the ceremony is rounded off, when all the swans have been put back into the river, by a ducking for one of the crew.

The other occasion is the Doggett Coat and Badge Race, an esoteric sporting event run by the Fishmongers for Watermen. It is the longest, oldest and toughest race for single sculls in the world, taking place over a four and a half mile stretch of river from the Swan at London Bridge to the Swan at Chelsea. It was instituted by a Fishmonger, Irish actor and comedian called Thomas Doggett, to commemorate the accession of George I to the throne of Great Britain in 1714. The race is held in July on the anniversary of the accession of the House of Hanover, and the prize is a silver cup, coat and badge provided by the Fishmongers out of the Doggett bequest. The participants, apart from being able to row, must also have completed their apprenticeship to the Watermen's Company. Formerly, when the race was rowed against the tide, it took four to five hours and eventually became too exhausting for both rowers and spectators, so now it is rowed with the tide and par for the course is about twenty-five minutes. It is umpired by the Bargemaster of the Fishmongers, himself a Doggett, who is dressed for his important task in gold-braided coat and cocked hat. Former winners of the race, known as Doggett Coat and Badge Men, help to organize the flotilla of motor launches bearing the spectators, and, keen rowing men that they are, they also take a professional interest in the race. After it is over the exhausted contestants are left panting on Cadogan Pier while the liverymen, their wives and guests return by water to the Fishmongers Hall for lunch. The official presentation to the winner takes place in November, by which time a new Coat and Badge will be ready for him. On this occasion all forty-five living Doggetts are invited to the Fishmongers Hall to dine with the livery of the Company. After the dinner is over the new man is led into the hall, accompanied by the inevitable trumpet fanfare. The Master presents him with a silver cup and congratulates him on admission to this body of men which, limited as it is to winning rowing Watermen, is one of the most exclusive in the world.

Doggett Coat and Badge Men are to the Fishmongers Hall almost what the Beefeaters are to the Tower of London. At all big livery dinners, they line the staircase, dressed in scarlet eighteenth-century-style oarsmen's costumes, each armed with an oar. Their ceremonial potential is further exploited by enterprising banqueting managers of one or two expensive London hotels, who when wishing to add an extra ceremonial flourish to a traditional dinner, get the Doggett Coat and Badge men to carry in the baron of beef on their stalwart shoulders.

London is a city which thrives on ceremonial, although the resulting congestion sometimes creates transport problems. Parades and processions always brought chaos to the city's packed thoroughfares, but today they also bring a bit of the colourful past into the motor-dominated present. From the grand annual spectaculars like the State Opening of Parliament and the Lord Mayor's Show, to quaint medieval leftovers like the biennial Beating of the Bounds, there are innumerable occasions when tradition triumphs over traffic. The Livery Companies' part in London's ceremonial life is not as splendid as the horse-drawn majesty of the State, nor as thrilling as the armoured might of the military, but when they show their public face, dressed in their multi-coloured liveries and carrying sweetly scented posies, they contribute a gentle civic dignity almost as impressive.

Chapter 6

Charities

a nursery of charities and a seminary of good citizens.
From the Minutes of the Grocers Company, 18 August 1687

One of a Livery Company's earliest concerns was the care of needy freemen, and this gradually developed into a more wide-spread charitable consideration for the poor in general; through all the changes encountered over the centuries the Companies have clung most tenaciously to this original charitable role and today their almsgiving continues unabated. The preservation of their valuable possessions and whimsical life-style are therefore less important to them than the task of administering their charitable funds.

Although they are modest and reticent about the amounts they give away, the combined annual sum puts them with the Carnegie Corporation and the Nuffield Foundation among the top charitable bodies in the world. Individually the money each Company can spare varies so enormously that it is quite impossible to generalize, although all Companies attempt to give something; the contributions of some of the impoverished Minor Companies are akin to the widow's mite, but among the Great Twelve gifts run into thousands of pounds a year.

A Livery Company has two sources of wealth. One is its corporate property, derived from investments made by the Company and land or money given to it outright by individual benefactors. The other is its trust properties: land or money given or bequeathed to the Company, the income from which must be used to support certain charitable foundations. For many the income from these trust funds is now considerably greater than that from their corporate funds and so, although they appear to have a lot of money to spend, it is very strictly controlled by the terms of the bequest. Corporate funds once the proper taxes have been paid, on the other hand, are unrestricted and as financially private bodies the Companies are entitled to spend them how they please. Corporate or trust funds are largely

A carved wood poor box belonging to the Coachmakers and Coach Harness Makers. Dated 1680 it has full length figures at each corner and bears the names of the Master and Wardens of the Company for the year it was made.

151

derived from investments in land and property over the past centuries. The high cost of every square foot of office space in the City of London has brought wealth beyond the dreams of avarice not only to many property speculators, but also to the Livery Companies. Due to the practice at the end of the nineteenth century of selling land to developers on a ninety-nine-year lease, some Companies have recently been enriched overnight by the falling in of a lease. While a developer reaped the financial reward from the properties he had erected, the Company who owned the lease might only receive some £1,500 per annum from the ground rent; but on expiry after ninety-nine years the whole reverts once more to the owner and the piece of land is suddenly transformed into a golden goose laying eggs to the tune of £100,000 per annum. Thus some Companies who have a serious income position today nevertheless have enormous capital prospects can they but hold on until a valuable lease falls in.

At a time when the funds that the Livery Companies have inherited for the alleviation of human suffering are growing at a spectacular rate, the need for charity would seem to be diminishing. What should they do with the money? If we assume that there is no such thing as destitution today, that the welfare state has ensured that no child shall grow up illiterate, that no old man shall starve to death and no one seriously ill lack hospital care, then it might seem that the role of the Livery Companies as charitable bodies is superfluous. But poverty is always relative and the State tends to provide only the minimum. Livery Companies therefore spend a good deal in supplementing the State's parsimony and in easing individual cases of hardship which have fallen through the State's security net. The changing social needs of each century present these Companies with the task of adapting their ancient funds to meet different problems, though as innovators they tend to be a little conservative. This may be because their current decisions are apt to be inhibited by the weight of tradition attached to the bequests they have to administer.

But some of the rich benefactors who founded these charities made their fortunes on risk and speculation. Maybe at the end of their lives they regretted the financial piracy which had made them what they were and, worrying about their reception in the next world, attempted to balance the account with some spectacular aid for the poor. Whatever the spiritual outcome, they certainly bought immortality for themselves on earth. Names such as Andrew Judd, Benjamin Kenton, Robert Aske, William Jones, Francis Bancroft, or Christopher Boone would long since have been forgotten but for the charity which now perpetuates their memory. One name, however, that needs no charitable foundation to be guaranteed immortality is that of Dick Whittington. It is strange that of all the colourful characters who have fought their way to mayoral office, Richard Whittington should have the monopoly of nursery fable and pantomime. He was not the poorest, the richest, nor the best. That he became the symbol of a medieval success story may have been because he had the kind of personality and charisma which breeds a legend, that he was the sort of man who could make at Thomas Spital (St Thomas's Hospital) in the fifteenth century

> a new chamber with 8 beds for young women that had done amiss in trust of a good mendment. And he commanded that all the things that be done in that chamber should be kept secret with out forth, in pain of losing their living, for he would not shame no young woman in no wise for it might be cause of her letting [preventing] of her marriage.

In fact Richard Whittington had a comfortable and respectable start in life, though he certainly increased his fortune and was Lord Mayor four times altogether. But a good tale needs a little embellishment. The poor boy arriving in London with nothing but a black cat and a few possessions to look for streets paved with gold is but legendary gilt on the gingerbread: the real story lies in what happened to Whittington's money when he died in 1424. In his will he left a piece of ground beside his house in the City on which to build an almshouse for thirteen men or women who were poor citizens of London, which he endowed with land and money from the bulk of his fortune and entrusted to the Mercers on the death of his executors. The value of the whole at that time was about £6,000. Over the centuries the almshouses have sheltered countless poor folk, been rebuilt several times and expanded. In spite of the considerable annual cost of such a charitable foundation, the income from the money is still growing and is now almost £100,000 per annum. 550 years after Whittington's death the old legend seems rather apt, for the land he left in the City of London has indeed turned into gold.

There was nothing new in Richard Whittington's almshouse idea. Sometimes known as colleges or hospitals, these 'dwellings of noble poverty' have provided roofs over the heads of the deserving poor ever since King Althelstone built the first almshouse in York in the ninth century. It is a measure of the consistency of human plight that they are still necessary, and today there are two and a half thousand separate groups of almshouses in this country. An almshouse is a dwelling provided for the aged poor by a charitable trust, the occupants of which are licensees of the trustees as opposed to tenants. Care of the aged has always been a major Livery Company concern and today eighteen Companies still maintain almshouses from

The Mercers' mace. It is in the form of a crowned maiden, the Company's symbol and is cast solid. This is one of a pair made for the Company in 1679 at a cost then of £29 5s.

their charitable funds. Some Companies with limited resources and poorer freemen maintain their almshouses exclusively for the benefit of their own members. The Watermen for instance have just completed the rebuilding of fifty semi-detached cottages in a magnificent setting in Hastings where retired Watermen and Lightermen can pass their remaining years; the Carpenters have almshouses at Twickenham and Godalming for poor freemen or widows of decayed freemen of the Company; the Bakers, Brewers, Weavers and Framework Knitters all have almshouses to take care of those members of their Companies who have nowhere to go in their old age. It must be one of the cheapest and pleasantest forms of insurance to join a Livery Company at the peak of prosperity, enjoy many years of companionship and conviviality and know that, should evil times befall, there is the chance of a rent-free home at the end of the day in one of the Company almshouses. Many people still believe that Livery Companies only provide help for their own poor freemen. But in fact since 1424, when Whittington left his almshouses for any poor citizen of London, their benevolence has been available to any in need. Companies such as the Mercers, Drapers, Fishmongers, Skinners, Merchant Taylors, Haberdashers, Ironmongers, Salters, Vintners, Dyers, Girdlers and Leathersellers all provide almshouse accommodation to any who through age, ill-health, accident, misfortune or infirmity are unable to maintain themselves by their own exertions.

Almshouses are made up of self-contained units consisting of a bed or bedsitting room, kitchenette and bathroom, one large 'common room', and laundry facilities. They have a resident matron, warden or 'tutor', to keep an eye on the old people and be within call of buzzers should anyone have a queer turn in the night or seize up in their bath. Some Companies charge a minimal rent, which in cases of need can be recouped from the State; others take care of everything—rent, rates, lighting and heating and in addition issue a small weekly cash payment.

The architectural style of the buildings varies from the beautiful and ancient to streamlined modern. A great many almshouses have been rebuilt since the war and nearly all the others have had to be modernized. Some were badly bombed, or became impracticable, others stood in the way of redevelopment. Many companies sold valuable city sites and moved their almshouses to the country; others were already in the country because the lands originally bequeathed were the country estates of the donors. One of the problems for those who have had to move out is that their accommodation is no longer where the greatest need is. Old people develop very strong ties to locality and possessions. The Drapers Company who have almshouses at Southwark, Tottenham, Greenwich and Wokingham have very long waiting lists for the London ones, but nobody born within the sound of Bow Bells wants to go and live in beautiful Berkshire and be frightened stiff by the silence.

The new almshouses are not very different from the old in their overall concept. They still contain little independent units within one complex, all under the vigilance of warden or matron. Perhaps the most comfortable almshouses to be erected since the war are those built by the Mercers under the Whittington Trust. In 1962 they had to move from their old site in Highgate, because of the Archway Road intersection, and so were rebuilt outside East Grinstead. There twenty-eight old ladies live in a village within a village at Felbridge. Each one has a living room, two bedrooms, kitchen and bathroom with central heating and hot water. There is a chapel to seat forty-eight people, equipped with hearing aids, as well as the usual ecclesiastical accessories. There are houses for the tutor, the matron, the assistant matron and the gardener, a fully equipped laundry and a dispensary. Overlooking it all is the statue of the benefactor, Richard Whittington. Any widow or spinster over the age of fifty-five living anywhere in the United Kingdom who is a communicant member of the Church of England is eligible and selection is entirely according to need.

Others are still in the original old buildings, beautiful period almshouses like the Fishmongers' picturesque Elizabethan houses at Bray, or the Mercers' charming seventeenth-century hospital at Greenwich. Trinity Hospital was begun by Henry Howard, Earl of Northampton, for poor men of Greenwich and bequeathed to the Mercers in 1614, though Northampton was not a member of the Company. Twenty-one old men live in modernized self-contained little flats within the creeper covered framework of the original building. The staircases are the original ones of 1616, the panelled court room is unmarked by bomb or beetle. It is rather like a small Oxford college, with its serene inner courtyard and small simple chapel. The gardens are the pride of the assistant warden's heart and are frequently first in the London Almshouse Garden Competition. A mulberry tree planted in James I's reign still flourishes among the roses, bearing large purple berries in late summer.

The Goldsmiths and Clothworkers Companies contribute to the supply of homes through housing trusts. The Clothworkers give financial help to the Hanover Housing Association, and the Goldsmiths have their own housing trust, which was formed in 1953 and has built forty-eight flats near the Company almshouses at Acton. In 1957 the Company let the almshouses to the trust, which has since improved them and is rebuilding a further thirty-two.

Very modern almshouses built in 1970 by the Skinners Company at Palmers Green. These replace the nineteenth century almshouses which were seriously damaged by fire in 1966.

The Livery Companies are more than adequately looking after a large number of old people who are independent, providing a home where they can keep their possessions around them, and daily contact with a warden, who can call a doctor should they be taken ill. What none of them so far has faced up to is the problem of what becomes of their almspeople when they are no longer able to look after themselves. From the simple problems of dressing or feeding themselves to the full care of the bedridden, there is no solution in an almshouse. The Livery Companies provide accommodation and community spirit but so far nothing more; at the moment, when the almspeople need nursing care their only alternative is a geriatric ward. Since there is no cure for old age, it is wasteful for them to occupy valuable bedspace in up-to-date and expensively equipped hospitals. What they need is plenty of comfort and attention, but not all the wonders of modern medical science. Though many companies recognize the problem, the Mercers are the first to pioneer a remedy. With the vast resources of Whittington's trust behind them, they are preparing to grasp the nettle and to become responsible for their almspeople to the grave. At the cost of a quarter of a million pounds they are building an extra care unit at Felbridge, designed to cater for the needs of their old people when they are incapable of looking after themselves. It necessarily has to be a dual purpose unit. Plans have been made for fourteen bedsitting rooms and bathrooms for the frail and ambulent. Meals will be provided and the bedsitting rooms, with the adroit manoeuvring of some portable partitions, can be converted into a nursing wing for the bedridden. As they do not know how many will be frail and ambulent and how many bedridden at any given time, obviously they have to be as flexible as possible. They are, however, planning to take people from all their almshouses and not only those at Felbridge. The lessons they learn from this expensive experiment should help others who are trying to cope with the problem of old age. With the joint resources at their disposal, it should be possible for other Livery Companies to join forces to follow the Mercers' lead and build a similar unit between them to care for helpless old people from the various almshouses under their administration.

The Innholders instead of almshouses built two old people's homes, one in Wimbledon and the other in Tunbridge Wells, which cater for twenty-four old people in each and have a sick bay should any become bedridden. These are run by the Distressed Gentlefolk's Aid Society. The Carpenters run a convalescent home for working men in Rustington, Sussex, which was founded by Sir Henry Harben, a past Master of the Company, in 1897.

Another charitable field in which liverymen have been most active is education. Land and money left for almshouses often would include the bequest of a free school for poor boys, almost as an afterthought. The Haberdashers, who now have interests in eight schools, were bequeathed them by former liverymen in the seventeenth century: William Jones in 1613 gave the Company £6,000 to found almshouses for twenty poor people and to provide a preacher at Monmouth, and a further £3,000 to establish a 'free school'; Robert Aske left the Haberdashers in 1688 £20,000 with which to buy a piece of land within one mile of London and to build on it an almshouse for twenty poor unmarried freemen of the Company and for the establishment of a school for twenty boys who were the sons of poor freemen; William Adams in 1656 gave the Company his land in Staffordshire for the foundation of a free grammar school and four almshouses in the town of Newport, Salop; Thomas Aldersey founded a free grammar school at Bunbury, appointed the Master and four Wardens of the Haberdashers as governors and left in support of this school great and small tithes of Bunbury and several other towns in the county of Cheshire. But not all the Livery Company schools were founded by their own liverymen. Eminent outsiders also recognized the potential of the guilds as trustees of integrity. The first school to be given to a Livery Company was St Paul's, founded by John Colet, Dean of St Paul's, in the fifteenth century. It was richly endowed with lands in the City, Stepney and Buckinghamshire, and entrusted to the Mercers in the Dean's will dated 1512. Colet's friend Erasmus describes the transaction in a letter to Justus Jones: 'After he [Colet] had finished all, he left the perpetual care and oversight of the estate and government of it—not to the Clergy, not to the Bishop, not to the Chapter, not to any great Minister at Court—but amongst married laymen, to the Company of Mercers, men of probity and reputation', Erasmus goes on to describe the reasons Colet gave for choosing a guild: 'that there was no absolute certainty in human affairs but for his part he found less corruption in such a body of citizens than in any order or degree of mankind.'

The Fishmongers were bequeathed a school in 1555 by John Gresham, who was in fact a Mercer, brother of Thomas Gresham. But the Mercers already had St Paul's School and Thomas was leaving them a great deal of property including the Royal Exchange, so maybe John felt he would achieve more attention if he took his school elsewhere. Others schools like Oundle, Tonbridge and Aldenham which are now well-known boys' public schools were all founded in the sixteenth century by philanthropic liverymen and bequeathed to their respective Companies to administer. Sir Andrew Judd, a great merchant of the time and Master of the Skinners Company on six occasions, left the free grammar school which he founded in his

native Tonbridge to the Skinners, endowing it richly with house property in Gracechurch Street and fields in the parish of St Pancras; so richly in fact that the trust in the nineteenth century spawned another school in Tonbridge. Oundle was founded by Sir William Laxton, Lord Mayor in 1544 and Master of the Grocers eight times. Laxton may in fact have revived an old school rather than founded a new one, as there is evidence that there was a school in Oundle as early as Henry VII's reign. Aldenham was left to the Brewers Company by Richard Platt. The only school to have been founded entirely by a Company itself is Merchant Taylors School, which was founded in 1561 by the Master (Richard Hilles), Wardens and Court of Assistants out of the Company's corporate funds 'for the better education and bringing up of children in good manners and literature'.

The founding of a school in the sixteenth century was a fairly simple task, the most important part being tying up the land and endowments in a charter or by letters patent, in case subsequent governments might be tempted to seize them. Then the only buildings considered necessary were a schoolroom, and a house each for a master and an usher. During the time of the Companies' prosperity the schools benefited from their interest and financial help, but, in the difficult years of the seventeenth century and in the inertia of the eighteenth, some schools suffered badly from neglect; then the roles were reversed and Companies did not scruple to use some of the endowment money to help them in their adversity. By the nineteenth century things were better. Some remarkable masters, such as F. W. Sanderson at Oundle, put fresh life into them and laid the foundations for their present position as great public schools. But the type of education received was not always very suitable to the kind of children who attended the school. The Court of the Haberdashers visiting Monmouth School in 1827 commented on its unsuitable syllabus: 'The present Masters, though so liberally paid and having so little to do, consider themselves engaged only to teach Latin and Greek. A school teaching those branches of learning only will never be useful to a place of such confined population as Monmouth.' Like poor Tom Tulliver, who was sent to the Reverend Snelling for 'an eddication as'll be a bread to him' and only received from the diligent clergyman a strong dose of Eton grammar and Euclid, so the sons of local tradesmen attending the free grammar schools were being fed an unrelieved diet of classics which benefited them little commercially. In schools such as Monmouth and Oundle the battle between gentlemanly learning and a useful education was eventually solved by the introduction of a two-tiered system—a high-grade classical school, and a modern school suitable for the sons of the neighbouring farmers and traders.

The beautiful seventeenth century almshouses at Greenwich known as Trinity Hospital, which were founded by the Earl of Northampton for poor men of Greenwich in 1614. The trust is administered by the Mercers' and twenty-one old men now live in separate contained flatlets in peaceful seclusion.

The schools that had originally begun as free grammar schools for day boys were beginning by the nineteenth century to take a few fee-paying boarders. At first it was just a tendency on the part of impecunious masters to take sons of successful tradesmen for privately agreed fees. Then Thomas Arnold at Rugby transformed a tendency into a successful trend and the professional and business classes started sending their boys away to school instead of having expensive tutors at home. Some of the earliest Livery Company schools developed into fee-paying boarding schools in this way. In 1902 the Education Act imposed the responsibility for secondary education on local authorities and some Livery Company schools availed themselves of help from the State. Then in 1944 the Education Act reorganized the financial status of schools once again, and the managers of the Livery Companies' schools had to decide what part, if any, they would play in the state system. The result is that eight are totally independent, six accept a degree of help and the rest are virtually state schools, but subsidized by the Company to which they belong. Of the eight independent schools, there are the six boys' public schools founded in the sixteenth century: St Paul's (Mercers), Greshams (Fishmongers), Merchant Taylors, Tonbridge (Skinners), Oundle (Grocers) and Aldenham (Brewers); and two girls' public schools: St Paul's an off-shoot of the boys' school, established in 1903, and Howell's, which belongs to the Drapers and owes its establishment in 1859 to an extraordinarily complicated inheritance. The money came from funds which had originally been left to the Drapers Company by Thomas Howell in 1540, who directed his executors 'to send to the City of London to be delivered to the house named Drapers Hall 12,000 ducats of gold from Spain in trust to buy therewith 400 ducats of rent to be bestowed in marriage to four maidens every year for ever of his lineage if they could be found and if not to four other maidens of good name and fame' etc. Twenty-one free orphan foundationers, who represent the original beneficiaries of Howell's will, are supported at the school and they are each still entitled to a marriage portion of £100, some of which may be anticipated for further education or training on leaving school.

Those schools accepting a degree of help are direct grant schools, which are fee-paying but receive a grant from the Ministry of Education in return for taking a minimum of twenty-five per cent non-fee-paying pupils, for whom the local authorities may pay the fees. They are: Monmouth (Haberdashers), Bancroft (Drapers), a second Howell's school from the Howell foundation at Llandaff (Drapers), Dauntsey (Mercers) and Haberdashers Aske, Haberdashers Aske Girls' School and Monmouth Girls' School (Haberdashers).

The poor boys of the sixteenth century received a free education at these well-endowed schools, but what advantages can the fee-paying parent expect today? There is the occasional big bonus, like a new library or an arts centre, which can be paid for out of income from the endowments, instead of the money having to be raised from long-suffering parents or former pupils. In terms of facilities therefore parents get very good value for their money at such schools. There are also in most cases annual scholarships available for those in reduced circumstances. Aldenham, for instance, has four major scholarships a year, two from Richard Platt's original foundation and two more from other Brewers who later left money to the Company for this purpose. Other benefits are less tangible, like the continuity achieved by having members of the Court on the governing body. A school like Oundle, or Tonbridge, has its governing body entirely composed of the Members of the Court of the Company. Just as a club rugby team playing regularly together can be more effective than an international side composed of brilliant players unaccustomed to each other's technique, so such a governing body has the advantage over others because they are accustomed to working together. They meet once a week on Company business, whereas the governors of other schools may only see each other four times a year at school meetings. Masters and boys pay frequent visits to the hall and get to know their governors personally. Such a close-knit framework makes it easier for the governors to understand the school's problems and to steer it along the lines most advantageous to the interests of both teachers and taught.

The schools within the state system are eighteen voluntary aided schools linked with the Haberdashers, Mercers, Merchant Taylors, Dyers, Grocers, Skinners, Brewers, Clothworkers, Coopers, Leathersellers, Ironmongers and Stationers. They are secondary or primary, boys' or girls', grammar and even recently comprehensive, and none of them has fee-paying pupils. The running expenses are the responsibility of the local authorities but the Companies appoint two-thirds of the governing bodies and therefore control their respective schools and in return have to bear twenty per cent of the cost of external maintenance of all capital improvements. The Brewers, for instance, who had two schools in Islington, established under the will of Dame Alice Owen—a boys' school in 1613 and a girls' school in 1878—have recently rebuilt them as a combined modern comprehensive school at Potters Bar. The Skinners have been similarly up to date with their girls' school at Stamford Hill.

Nor is it only Companies who inherited schools hundreds of years ago who take an interest in the state schools today. The Dyers, for instance, decided shortly after the war that they

A silver box by John Donald incorporating a medal won in 1893 for mathematics at Tonbridge. It was presented to the Skinners Company in 1964 by G. A. Hill, Master in 1953/54 and son of the prize winner.

wanted to take an interest in education so they decided to 'adopt' Norwich grammar school. Their financial help has been fairly substantial, including a new science block called the Fleming block after Sir Alexander Fleming who was an Honorary Dyer. The Tobacco Pipe Makers and Tobacco Blenders Company, since its revival in 1954, also wished to become interested in a school. The Company chose a school in Sevenoaks and from its benevolent fund now give scholarships, send pupils on courses on the Sir Winston Churchill sail training ship and other projects. The Saddlers Company came to the rescue when the Inner London Education Authority stopped providing free places at Alleyn's School and gave the school thirty 'Saddlers' scholarships' a year.

In addition to the money spent on schools the Companies are also very liberal in their support for universities. Chairs such as the English Chair at Oxford and the Economics Chair at Cambridge have been endowed by the Goldsmiths and Girdlers respectively. The Mercers, in addition to administering the large trusts of Whittington, Northampton and Colet, also administer money from Thomas Gresham, for instance. He left the Royal Exchange to the Mercers and the Corporation of London. The income was to be used partly to support seven persons to read public lectures in divinity, astronomy, music and geometry (these four to be appointed by the Corporation of London) and the law, physics and rhetoric (these three to be appointed by the Mercers). The lectures now are given at the new City University in St John Street. They are still open to the public but they are also attended by students of the university. Collectively the Livery Companies provide some fair-sized funds for educational grants – money for scholarships, exhibitions, awards, travel scholarships and exchange schemes. They have to be careful though to ensure that grants formerly made by them for educational purposes do not, if continued, have the effect of subsidizing the government's own grants in the same field. There are, however, still cases of hardship in education as elsewhere, which do not fit into the state scheme of benefits. The Skinners are filling a gap that they have recently found which has been caused by the fact that in the private sector the changeover from preparatory to secondary school takes place at the age of thirteen and in the state schools at the age of eleven plus. If, therefore, a boy in a state primary school wants to take a scholarship to a private public school he has a two-year gap to fill. The Skinners accordingly award, on academic merit and subject to a means test, a number of scholarships to bridge the gap for boys who live locally and intend to sit the scholarship examination for Tonbridge School at the age of thirteen. The field of education is complicated enough for the expert, let alone the bewildered parent, who seldom has a complete knowledge of all the various grants on offer. This is why the Goldsmiths and Drapers Companies in 1959 set up a voluntary body called the Educational Grants Advisory Service – a sort of poor man's Gabbitas and Thring. With the co-operation of the National Council of Social Service, EGAS freely advises parents and young people on where to seek help to overcome the financial obstacles in their chosen educational path.

Some funds available now for educational grants were not in fact originally intended as such. They were to relieve such things as slavery or imprisonment for debt, mishaps which fortunately no longer overtake people today. Until 1869, it was the custom to imprison a man who owed money until he paid his creditors. This harsh treatment had the practical effect of sentencing a debtor to life imprisonment, unless he had a friend who would pay his debts for him. Quite a few liverymen left trust funds for 'the release of poor prisoners', maybe having been close enough to the spectre of bankruptcy themselves to have a special sympathy for these poor unfortunates. When a charitable trust is no longer relevant the funds can be reallocated, after a great deal of legal red tape, to another deserving cause. One of the trusts of the Drapers Company which is now spent on help for secondary education for girls is made up of the amalgamated funds of bequests from six different liverymen who left money for the relief of poor prisoners.

One of the largest of the charities administered by the Ironmongers Company is that of Thomas Betton, who when he died in 1723 left half his considerable estate for the freeing of British slaves in Barbary and Turkey. There was no proof that Betton had actually had first-hand experience of the horrors of slavery until quite recently when a Master of the Company with a more than usually inquiring mind was browsing in the archives and discovered papers proving that Betton had indeed been a slave. Between the years 1734 and 1834 the Company spent £21,000 of Betton's trust rescuing 135 Britons from the barbarous Turk. With the abolition of slavery the Ironmongers then had a problem of what to do with the money. Before they could use it for other charitable purposes the sanction of the Court of Chancery had to be obtained. Litigation took twelve years and went to the House of Lords, before finally the Company were allowed to spend that part of Betton's trust which had applied to the redemption of slaves on educational purposes for Church of England schools in England and Wales.

There are, however, some trusts which, though they may seem somewhat old fashioned today, have remained unchanged. These are a number of ancient trusts providing for the preaching of sermons. The Armourers have such a sermon on St George's Day, and the Haberdashers, Salters, Skinners, Merchant Taylors, Cordwainers and Mercers all still have sermons

Porters staffhead of the Drapers, which was given them by Thomas Hardwick in 1773. The crowned figure of the Virgin Mary is supported by two angels.

preached on certain days as a result of ancient bequests. The Stationers combine food for the body as well as the soul at their 'Cakes and Ale Sermon' on Ash Wednesday. In 1612 Alderman John Norton left money to the Company to provide a sermon in St Faith's under St Paul's on Ash Wednesday and to supply 'cakes and ale' after the service, presumably to revive them after the rigours of the sermon. Formerly the ale was a special brew and the cakes home made; the Company still parade to St Paul's to hear their annual Ash Wednesday sermon and afterwards return to their hall where they enjoy Alderman John Norton's hospitality with Truman's rich black ale and ABC cakes.

A number of Companies still hold the advowsons of a variety of churches—the Haberdashers are patrons of eleven livings, the Grocers also have eleven and the Mercers six. In practice this means that not only do the Companies choose a vicar for the parish, but they also help with repairs to the church, his salary and any charitable initiatives he might undertake. For instance the Grocers were responsible for appointing to the Church of St Stephen Walbrook in 1954 the Reverend Chad Varah who subsequently founded the Samaritans' organization. Its headquarters are in the crypt of the church and the Company provided the sum of £14,000 towards the cost of building the necessary premises.

If social progress has made some charitable bequests obsolete, inflation has made the degree of relief offered by others absurd. For centuries the Companies have been accumulating little bequests from countless benefactors, all designed to leave a meticulously specified annual sum in perpetuity to widows, orphans, decayed freemen, pure maidens, poor lame painters, poor maimed soldiers, blind persons over fifty or poor clergymen. The Cooks Company have to remember to distribute good black tea to all the widow pensioners of the Company once a year with money left them by W. S. Angell in 1842; the Poulterers still administer the Thomas and Ann Neptun trust which involves the Company in a visit to Barking and Ilford once a year when they distribute £1.50 each to eighty old men and women. The amounts specified in such trusts bear no relation to the purchasing power of the pound today. Five pounds a year to sustain a poor curate in the sixteenth century may have made all the difference between starvation and survival then, but it would do little more than buy him a piece of roast beef for his Sunday dinner now. It is therefore impracticable for all these trusts to be carried out individually. Since the 1960 Charities Act it has become easier to extend the 'cy pres' doctrine, which permits alternative uses related to the original purpose. Many Companies have gone along to the Charity Commissioners and had their innumerable small sums lumped into one general charity whereby the Company can then interpret the spirit of the donor's intentions, uninhibited by the letter of the will. The money still goes to the poor, the old and the sick, the blind or the disabled, but in amounts that can be of real use to them.

In order to achieve effective relief the Companies sometimes have to top up their inherited charities with money from their own corporate funds. Nowadays it is the goal of every Company to have its own trust fund in addition to the inherited trust funds it administers on behalf of long dead donors. Quincentenary celebrations can be used to start the ball rolling. This is how the Ironmongers launched their Company charitable fund, and in 1974 the Pewterers have a new Company fund to celebrate their five hundredth anniversary. The Minor Companies struggle along with small benevolent funds, whose main sources of income are the contributions of members and small fundraising operations; the Guild of Air Pilots' Benevolent Fund had a profitable and unusual start, based on the royalties from the memoirs of their first Master, Sir Sefton Brancker. The money Companies can produce out of their funds varies from two to three hundred pounds a year to one or two hundred thousand pounds a year.

There is no restriction on how money in a Company's own charitable fund should be spent, as long as it is for charitable purposes, and the Companies receive literally thousands of appeals every year. Opinion varies as to whether it is better to spread the butter thinly to help the greatest number of people a little, or to direct lump sums to make a greater impact with a few. The Companies with great sums at their disposal resist the temptation to pour it into one channel in the hope of achieving some spectacular cure for human ills. But the Clothworkers did have a coup in 1947 as a result of the exchange scheme between Guys Hospital and the John Hopkins medical school in Baltimore, which they initiated in 1946 as a thanksgiving scheme on the termination of the war. One of the first doctors the scheme brought to this country was Dr Alfred Blalock, who introduced his technique for cardiac operations known as the 'blue baby' operation. His sponsored visit resulted in a clinic being instigated for the treatment of congenital heart cases where British surgeons have carried on the treatment which Dr Blalock pioneered.

On the whole Companies play safe in supporting already established charitable bodies with sizable contributions. The Goldsmiths for instance give one large sum of about £60,000 to a specific project each year, and spread the rest, in grants varying from £500 to £5,000, among work for underdeveloped countries, the disabled, museums, libraries, the arts, housing, youth, the mentally handicapped and medical research. The Drapers spend £200,000 a year on widely varying charitable objects, including medical research, culture, the old, the young, the poor, almshouses and education. The Grocers spread a slightly smaller sum over a similarly well-balanced list of good causes.

Although the welfare state might have made the Livery Companies' charitable role something of an anachronism, yet the unique constitution of these private corporations is still peculiarly suitable for the administration of large trust funds for the benefit of society. The government cannot experiment with public money as can the Livery Companies with their private resources. Pioneering is nothing new to them. The trust funds they inherit were left to them by men who were helping to alleviate the social disasters of their time. The fact that much of what they did has now been taken over by the State is a measure of their success. The problem now facing those whose business it is to manage these funds is to look for the areas of greatest need in contemporary society and by their imaginative philanthropy lead the way for State aid.

Chapter 7

Trade

Whatever their detractors may say many Livery Companies have made spectacular attempts in the last hundred years to play a more active part in trade matters. In fact it is unlikely that they could have held on to their present important position in the City through good works alone. The influence and power they are able to wield may be partly due to the large funds at their disposal, but another reason they are still taken seriously is because they take a practical interest in their trade.

Some Companies never completely lost control of their crafts; today they are still binding apprentices, examining candidates or exercising their ancient powers of search. Nor are these activities just feudal leftovers which have somehow lingered on into this century and been allowed to remain through a whimsical quirk in the legal system. The City Companies who still enjoy statutory powers over their trade have been deliberately allowed to continue because they are best fitted to do the job. The adaptation of old methods to fit modern practice is a popular British tendency, particularly prevalent in the City of London. There tradition marries well with progress and contributes to the City's indefinable mystique.

Recent developments within the Vintners Company illustrate how a Livery Company can play a useful part in the commercial life of the country. With Britain's entry into the Common Market somebody had to organize the wine industry to conform with EEC regulations. The task has been given not to a government department, nor to a trade body like the Wine and Spirit Association, but to the Worshipful Company of

Vintners, who have the knowledge, the trade connections and the capacity to undertake the task.

But before this the Vintners were already playing an active part in the wine trade, lending their hall for meetings of such bodies as the Wine and Spirit Education Trust, the Wine and Spirit Association, the Guild of Sommeliers or the Wine Development Board. In 1953 they were responsible for introducing a Master of Wine Examination to replace the old indenture system which takes a lot of the humbug out of the hot air talked about wine. There are under a hundred people in this country who are Masters of Wine and candidates not only have to pass a stiff theoretical examination, but also distinguish themselves in a severe practical test. A love of wine and a lifetime's experience of the grape is not enough to make a Master. To pass the very stringent tasting test devised by the Vintners Company requires a palate of such sensitivity that it can easily be blunted by too much consumption in pursuit of knowledge.

On 20th August 1973 the Vintners received a new charter charging the Company with just the same responsibilities of search and oversight as those in its first charter of 1364 and the Company is now expanding to embrace its medieval role. A new building is planned at Kennet Wharf on an old site which has come back into the Vintners' possession on the termination of the lease. The building will be a centre for the wine trade and is to be known as Five Kings House, in memory of the five kings whom the Vintners had the honour of entertaining all on the same day in the fourteenth century.

The Goldsmiths Company has been hall-marking gold and silver wares at Goldsmiths Hall for over six hundred years and is one of the few Companies whose ancient powers of search have never lapsed. The very word 'hall-mark' has now become a synonym for high quality. The principle was established in 1300 by Edward I, who originally vested the right of assay in the Company, directing that no vessels of gold or silver should leave the maker's hand till they had been tested by the Wardens and stamped with the leopard's head. The first Office of Assay was established at the beginning of the fourteenth century and today there are three other Assay Offices, in Birmingham, Sheffield and Edinburgh, as well as the prototype at Goldsmiths Hall in London. All items which come to the London Assay Office, except foreign plate imported since 1904, are still marked with the leopard's head, the oldest of marks in origin and probably taken from the royal arms. The number of articles submitted to the Company for hall-marking in a year is over six-million, with more gold items than silver. However, the rise in the volume of silver wares in the past few years has been spectacular and the increasing amount of work is begin-

ning seriously to stretch the space available at Goldsmiths Hall for the Assay Office. Hall-marks refer to the quality of the metal and no piece is hall-marked until a sample of it has been subjected to accurate chemical analysis. If it is gold the quantity of precious metal is measured in carats: 22, 18, 14 or 9; if it is silver it may be either Britannia (.958) or sterling (.925). The standard of the metal having been assayed the piece is then marked with the date letter, the maker's and the Goldsmiths' mark.

The Goldsmiths Company test does not stop short at gold and silver articles but includes the coinage of the realm. The ancient custom by which the Company test the nation's pence is known as the Trial of the Pyx and the Goldsmiths have actual records of the proceedings from 1604, although the first known writ for a trial dates from 1280. The purpose of the trial is to provide an independent check on the accuracy of composition and weight of coins minted during the year. The Officers of the Mint during the course of the year place in the pyx (or Mint box) a sample of gold, silver and cupro-nickel coins which have been recently minted. Then on an appointed day the pyx box is taken to Goldsmiths Hall for trial. A jury of freemen of the Goldsmiths Company are sworn in by the Queen's Remembrancer and they count the representative sample of currency in the pyx box. The coins are weighed and a number reserved for assay. The trial is then adjourned to allow time for the necessary tests to be carried out. After about two months the jury reassembles at Goldsmiths Hall, with the Chancellor of the Exchequer attending in his capacity as Master of the Mint. The jury's verdict on the coinage is read by the Clerk of the Company and the occasion is celebrated with an excellent lunch.

London hallmark on silver 1584. It shows the date letter (G), sterling silver mark (Lion passant), London town mark (Goldsmiths' crowned leopard's head) and the maker's initial (I.C.)

The Goldsmiths are also concerned with the authenticity of old silver and gold objects. The Antique Plate Committee, consisting of a panel of experts, assist the Court in weeding out pieces of antique gold and silver plate which contravene the hall-marking laws. In spite of the fact that the Goldsmiths have been hall-marking silver and gold since 1300, much plate has still slipped through the net. In the eighteenth century a duty of 6d an ounce was imposed on finished wares, payable when the goods were assayed, which gave rise to some ingenious duty dodging. A common method was to send a small piece for assay and marking and then to insert the section into the base of a cup or bowl, a practice that even today makes such antiques illegal. In the course of a year the Committee meets six times and suspected articles which have been withdrawn from auction rooms and elsewhere are examined. Some 245 articles might be condemned in a year and whenever possible brought within the law by assay and hall-marking.

As well as assaying the composition of the actual metal, the Company is also concerned with encouraging high standards of design and craftsmanship. Its patronage for struggling young silversmiths has 'set' many a young man 'on work'. One of the greatest difficulties young designers encounter when they have completed their apprenticeship is obtaining commissions which are sufficiently ambitious for them to be able to show what they can do. The Company organizes competitions from time to time for important pieces of presentation plate; it also presents to any new university a piece of silver or gold worth £2,000 commissioned from a young silversmith embarking on his career. Many a prospering silversmith owes his now established position to the Goldsmiths for their help in getting him over his early hurdles. The beauty and quality of English gold and silver work is the Company's reward. So the Goldsmiths, one in four of whose members is actively engaged in the trade, are still fulfilling their ancient role. Among the livery there are enough designers, technical advisers, antique connoisseurs and craftsmen to man the many committees the Company needs to do its work of encouragement and research.

The Fishmongers are concerned not so much with aesthetics as with public health. Although there are not many of its members actually engaged in selling fish today, the Company still exercises its ancient power of search by the daily inspection of all fish sold in Billingsgate market. Two to four hundred tons of fish come daily into the City and process through the market into the shops and restaurants of London and the south east. Between the hours of six and nine in the morning the vicinity of Billingsgate reverberates with the rumbling of the fish porters' trolleys on the slippery cobblestones and the air reeks with the smell of a hundred different sorts of fish. Eels from Canada,

Early morning at Billingsgate Market. One of the Fishmongers' two Fishmeters inspecting fish for sale in the market. The Fishmongers daily exercise their ancient right of search of between 200 and 400 tons of fish which pass through the City by way of Billingsgate.

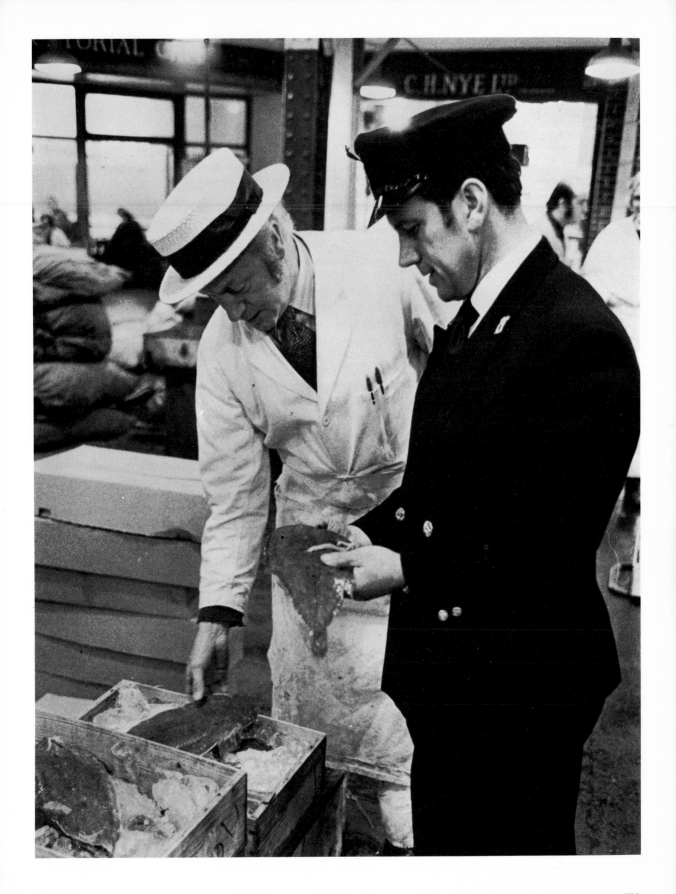

flying fish from Barbados, carp bred in captivity in France, live lobsters and oysters in their special tanks with circulating water, boxes of sole, halibut, hake, flounders and the more plebeian cod, all come under the keen surveillance of a Fish Inspector and his two assistants. The condition of this fishy tonnage has been the concern of the Fishmongers Company ever since James I's reign, when they were given the right to 'survey wither the same be wholesome for Man's Body, and fit to be sold or no'. The 'Fishmeters', as the Company's officials are called, are something of a cross between mentor and benevolent adviser. They do not sniff, prod and feel every cold-blooded vertebrate for sale, but tour the market two or three times each morning and their presence alone acts as a fairly effective deterrent. Although the Fish Inspector's walk around the market might appear a mainly social exercise, out of the corner of his eye he can always spot a poor fish when he sees one. When a fish is condemned it is stamped with an indelible red marker and sold to the maggot farmers to feed their hungry grubs. Some two to three hundred tons of fish a year are condemned, and the spoilage is due more to merchants holding on to their stock in the hope of getting a better price than to the poor quality of catches arriving in London; for the price of freight is now too high to make it worth taking a chance on sending a catch in dubious condition. If a Fishmeter sees fish losing their first freshness while waiting for a better price, he will have a fatherly word with the vendor and tell him not to have the same fish on sale again; the wise fish merchant will then sell his depreciating stock to the highest bidder while he has the chance. However, where a fish is really off the Fishmeters are less lenient and can condemn at a stroke a whole box of fish, which could represent a loss of some £70 for the poor merchant if it was an expensive fish like sole.

The Fishmongers exercise their right of search so efficiently that trainee public health inspectors and students on special courses from abroad come to Fishmongers Hall for instruction in fish inspection. Supervision at Billingsgate also keeps the Company in close touch with their trade and the Fishmeters' daily conversation with the dealers there provides information 'straight from the horse's mouth' which is of help to the Company in their other piscatorial interests. The conservation of salmon, research on bacteria in shellfish and on river pollution are some of the ways in which the Company involves itself in the trade. In 1907 it founded the Oyster Merchants and Planters Association to look after the interests of those concerned with oysters. The popularity of other crustacea made the Association widen the scope of its activities and it was renamed the Shellfish Association of Great Britain. Nor does the Company neglect the sporting element in the business of catching fish. In 1903 it formed the Salmon and Trout Association which

The proofmaster of the Gunmakers Company reading the barrels of a shot-gun for signs of damage or defects in the tubes, after provisional proof.

meets at Fishmongers Hall and protects the interests of keen fly fishermen. The Company also supports the Anglers' Co-operative Association and is a founder member of the National Anglers' Council.

Safety is the chief concern of the Gunmakers Company, who have held the right of 'view, gauge, proof, trial and marking of all hand-guns' ever since their royal charter of incorporation in 1637, and the Company's seventeenth-century powers were consolidated in the Gun Barrel Proof Acts of 1868 and 1950. All guns for sale in this country, except those destined for Her Majesty's Forces, still have to be proved either at the Gunmakers' Proof House in London, the oldest in the world, or at the Birmingham Proof House, which was established by Act of Parliament in 1813. Guns from certain European countries who have their own proof houses, like France, Belgium, West

Germany, Italy and Spain, are accepted by the British authorities, but guns from countries such as the United States, who have no such legislation, have to be proved in this country before they can be offered for sale. The proving of a gun involves the firing through the barrel of a considerably heavier load than is customary in the shooting field, thereby putting a far greater strain upon the weapon than any imposed by standard load cartridges. This excessive pressure discloses any weakness in a gun, whether new or used, and is much better discovered at a Proof House than in the field.

The Proof House of the Gunmakers Company is a little square building in the Commercial Road without pretensions, distinguished only by the arms of the Company over the door and the smell of cordite hanging in the air. In the basement is the Company's court room. The long polished table and leather-backed chairs are characteristic of any Livery Company, but the pictures of famous gun makers, like Joseph Manton, and treasures like the rare 1814 Thomson breech loader around the walls could only belong to the Gunmakers. Everywhere else lining the walls and stacked upon the floor are guns. High-quality Purdeys for the American and world market, consignments of sub-machine guns, pistols, rifles, flare guns, industrial tools, humane killers, Japanese shot-guns, in fact every sort of firearm for private and commercial use waiting to be tested. Not only new guns but old ones which have been altered in any way have to return for proving before they can be sold. This poses something of a problem with antique firearms. Many collectors' pieces have long ago outlived the cartridges which were hand-made to fit their chambers; as it is therefore impossible to fire them they are certified for sale as 'unproofable'.

Methods of proving have changed little during the past three centuries and although modern equipment is used to make the task easier, there is no satisfactory substitute for the expertise of an experienced Proof Master. Guns are fired in underground rooms, which consist of a sand bunker, a cradle to hold the barrels and a simple mechanism for remote firing. Then the barrels are examined for any sign of weakness. It takes many years for a man to 'read' barrels accurately, but his task is helped by a little device called an introscope for inspecting the surfaces for signs of pitting.

Shot-guns are submitted twice for proving. The first time the gunsmith sends the barrels only for provisional proof, so that should they be faulty he is saved the otherwise considerable expense of fitting the action mechanism and stock. For this test the naked barrels are laid side by side in a bunker up to thirty at a time and ignited by a trail of gunpowder fired by remote control from outside. When the deafening explosion and acrid

A gun being impressed with definitive proof marks at the Gunmakers' Proof House in the Commercial Road. The majority of guns in use at the present time have been proved or reproved since 1925. Marks are normally made on the flats of shotgun barrels or otherwise near the breech and upon the action.

Parcel-gilt Beadle's staffhead, surmounted by the crest of the Cutlers Company dating about 1680.

smoke have cleared away, the barrels are cleaned and examined. Those that successfully pass the scrutiny are marked with a provisional proof mark and returned to the gunmaker. When the shot-gun next appears at the Proof House it has been fitted with the action and is ready for definitive proof. This time two empty cartridges are fitted into the chambers and filled with a carefully measured charge of shot and powder. The gun is then fixed to a cradle in one of the bunkers and fired. The barrels are then cleaned and examined once more. If all is in order the gun is finally marked with definitive proof, bore size (dimension of the barrel), nitro-proof mark, chamber length and pressure. Guns can easily become damaged by mishandling or weakened through neglect, and repairs may necessitate the enlarging of the barrels beyond the dimensions marked on them. In this case the gun has to be returned once more for proving. In the event of a gun not passing the test the original proof marks are defaced. Three million guns a year are sent to the Gunmakers Company for proving. The work is done by the Proof Master and his assistant, with the help of up to three probationers who are learning the technique.

Learning a trade the hard way is an unpopular method today, and the apprentice is a rare bird. The Watermen and Lightermen, who act as the licensing body for the Port of London Authority, still teach river craft in the time-honoured way and bind up to twenty apprentices a year. These lads begin, after the age of fourteen and before the age of twenty, with two years working on the river. Then they are examined in river craft at Watermen's Hall and if found satisfactory given an apprentice's licence. When they have served their time—which varies from between five and seven years—they come up before the Court of the Company again for a further examination which, if they pass, entitles them to ply their trade on the River Thames as Watermen and Lightermen and admits them to the freedom of the Company. The Cutlers maintain their interest in cutlery by fostering apprenticeships in the surgical instrument-making industry. Some thirty young men serving with the leading surgical instrument-making firms are apprenticed through the Cutlers Company. Once each year during their apprenticeship they have to exhibit specimens of their work to the Master, Wardens and Court of the Company and yearly prizes are awarded for merit. The Masons also encourage successful apprentices in stonemasonry with prizes to those who have done well in their examinations. Examinations have replaced the old 'master-piece' as an indication that the student has mastered his subject.

Anyone who has passed the Society of Apothecaries' examinations is recognized by the State as a fully qualified medical practitioner. In fact the development of the humble pharmacist into general medical practitioner gave birth to the family doctor. In the seventeenth and eighteenth centuries the surgeons and physicians were often too grand, too busy or too expensive for the ordinary citizens, who instead went round the corner to the apothecaries' shop and asked the man behind the counter for 'something for a bad stomach'. During the Great Plague in 1665, when many a prosperous physician fled the infectious city, the apothecaries proved their mettle by staying behind to do what they could to help the poor sufferers. Eventually the apothecaries found themselves providing free diagnosis and charging only for the medicines they sold. By the beginning of the nineteenth century many of them were educated men with a sound knowledge of medicine and the close touch they had developed with patients made them particularly suited to the pursuit of general medical practice. In those days when doctors made up their own medicines for their patients, prescribing was an art, but the knowledge of what to put into the medicines was almost as important.

In 1815 the Company acquired, under the Apothecaries Act, both the right to grant licences to practise medicine and the duty of controlling that practice. They dominated the medical field for the next fifty years by the stringency with which they applied their regulations and the reality of their apprenticeships. Doctors took the surgical diploma of the Royal College of Surgeons and the medical licence of the Apothecaries Society. Very few ever thought of making the effort to obtain the licence of the Royal College of Physicians.

Medical education in the nineteenth century owed a great deal to the Society's work of pioneering provincial medical schools, valuable botanical research in the famous Physic Garden at Chelsea and instruction in chemistry in its own laboratory at Apothecaries Hall. But the decline in apprenticeship and the rise of the great manufacturing drug houses at the end of the nineteenth century brought an end to the Apothecaries' domination. The Medical Act of 1886 which required evidence of qualification in medicine, surgery and midwifery before admission to the Medical Register, helped to bring the Royal College of Physicians back into the picture and they combined with the Royal College of Surgeons in granting a joint diploma. Today the Society's relations with the medical profession are confined chiefly to examining and licensing. Examinations are conducted in the Society's hall and in addition to its Licentiate in medicine and surgery (the LMSSA) the Society also examines for post-graduate diplomas in industrial health, medical jurisprudence and in the history and philosophy of medicine and pharmacy.

The Spectacle Makers Company has been examining opticians since 1898 when the Company first introduced its examination scheme. Since 1958 the Spectacle Makers diploma and dispensing certificate has been a compulsory qualification for all practising opticians. Now over a hundred candidates a year sit the Company's various examinations for ophthalmic, dispensing and craftsmen opticians at Apothecaries Hall.

Examinations and technical training have now replaced the traditional apprenticeship which worked so well in the past when the guilds controlled their own crafts. But the collapse of the old system was not immediately replaced by anything as thorough. By the 1850s Britain was lagging behind in technical education and the supremacy of the British-made article in world markets was being challenged by foreign competition. For years the country had coasted along on the high standards of workmanship achieved under the guild system. The binding of young men to master craftsmen had ensured a continual supply of skilled labour and the ruthless exercise of the powers of search had eliminated sub-standard products from the market. When the Industrial Revolution upset this system the need for technical know-how was just as important but the framework for handing on industrial knowledge was lacking.

By the end of the nineteenth century Mr Gladstone's public criticisms and rumblings of reform from his Liberal supporters chivvied the Livery Companies into making a come-back into technical education. In 1878 sixteen Companies, namely the Mercers, Drapers, Fishmongers, Goldsmiths, Salters, Ironmongers, Clothworkers, Dyers, Leathersellers, Pewterers, Armourers and Brasiers, Carpenters, Cordwainers, Coopers, Plaisterers and Needlemakers, together with the Corporation of London, jointly subscribed to the formation of the City and Guilds of London Institute for the Advancement of Technical Education. In 1900 the Institute's title was modified and became simply City and Guilds of London Institute and it was granted a royal charter. Other Companies, such as the Grocers, Skinners, Merchant Taylors, Vintners, Cutlers and Saddlers, supported the Institute and were fairly soon joined by many other Livery Companies and, under revised statutes allowed in 1958, there are now sixty-nine named Livery Companies included as 'founder members', whose total contribution over the years has amounted to some two million pounds.

The Council of the City and Guilds Institute realized that what industry needed was trained men in every grade from the craftsmen to the research scientist. They were therefore responsible for the setting up of three different types of training establishment: in 1879 the City and Guilds of London Arts School in Kennington in south-east London, which provided training in sculpture, carving, painting, drawing, etching and lettering; in 1882 the Finsbury Technical College, providing full-time and part-time courses in science and engineering which was the prototype of hundreds of technical institutions which have since proliferated all over the country; and in 1884 the Central Institution, providing the highest levels of teaching and research in engineering and science, which became the City and Guilds College and is now the Engineering Section of the Imperial College of Science and Technology, University of London. The Finsbury Technical College was closed down in 1926, having fulfilled its pioneering purpose.

The most important work of the City and Guilds Institute in this century has been the co-ordination of schemes for technical education throughout the country. It ensures that the educational services provide in terms of personnel what industry wants. The Institute has a close rapport with industry and expert antennae, in the form of a system of two hundred specialist committees, to identify educational needs. The practical application of all this knowledge is in the sort of examinations the Institute sets. Every year some 400,000 candidates sit the Institute's examinations on a wide range of subjects varying from the construction of highways to the analysis of knitting fabric. But you only get from exam results what you put into the questions. The Institute therefore takes very great care in getting the syllabuses right. It is constantly receiving requests from industry to introduce this scheme or that course to produce a different sort of manpower for a changing need. So the examiners have to maintain a flexible attitude to the courses they set, without thoroughly confusing all the educational bodies of the country who are trying to prepare their candidates for the final test.

Today the City and Guilds Institute has a turnover of two million pounds a year, which comes largely from examination fees. A non-profit-making organization, it is supported not only by subscriptions and donations from the Corporation of London and some fifty-five Livery Companies, but also by sums great and small from companies, trusts, societies, trade unions and associations. So technical training is big business.

In addition to what they contribute to the City and Guilds Institute, some Livery Companies also founded technical colleges of their own. One of the most important contributions to technical education has been that of the Clothworkers, who have been responsible for the entire department of textile industries at Leeds University. The Clothworkers started by giving financial support to the Yorkshire College of Science; then they gave a large grant for the building of a Department of Textile Industries at Leeds in 1874. Since then they have consistently supported the department, which became part of the University of Leeds in 1904, and now includes a colour chemistry and dyeing section and a new textile engineering department. The Company has not confined itself to the department alone, but provides large sums for hostels and other fringe benefits. Leeds University, which is one of the largest and most modern in England, also benefits from the Dyers, who contribute to the department of colour chemistry and dyeing; the Skinners, who give some support to the leather industries department; and the Woolmen, who present an annual scholarship of £40 to students engaged on research in wool.

The City of London has to thank the Livery Companies indirectly for their new university, which was once the Northampton Institute at Clerkenwell and was founded in 1891 by a group of City Companies including the Skinners and Saddlers. Meetings of the Council of the City University now take place at Skinners Hall and a member of their Court is Pro-Chancellor. The university has been fortunate in the christening presents it has received from its old founders—from the Saddlers a covered sports stadium for the use of the university staff and students, and from the Skinners a beautiful pair of modern silver-gilt standing cups and covers. London University has the Goldsmiths and the Drapers Companies to thank for two of its colleges—Queen Mary College, which used to be known as East London College and was established by the Drapers at a cost of some £500,000, and Goldsmiths College, which combines a teachers' training college and fine art school with an adult education department.

Technical colleges in building, tanning and shoemaking were all established around the turn of the century by Companies seeking once more a more direct involvement with their trades. The Building Crafts Training School in Great Titchfield Street was founded by the Carpenters and supported by them, with help from various other Companies such as the Joiners and Ceilers, the Masons, the Tylers and Bricklayers and the Pewterers. The school began modestly in 1893 as a wood-carving class but now teaches carpentry, joinery, masonry, plumbing and some welding. In 1966 the Carpenters Company decided to rebuild the school and modernize its facilities to provide training for mature tradesmen and supervisors as well as apprentices. It is thus developing into a National Craft University for the building industry as a whole. The Leathersellers' Technical College in Bermondsey, which was re-equipped and re-established as the National Leathersellers College in 1951, is one of the most up-to-date tanning schools in the world. The Cordwainers founded a college in Hackney which, with assistance from the London County Council and a little financial

A pair of large silver water jugs designed and made by Peter Musgrove in 1973. They are part of a gift of silver from the Goldsmiths Company to the University of East Anglia.

support from the Curriers, provides classes for four hundred students in the manufacture of boots, shoes and leather goods.

In 1918 the Salters founded the Institute of Industrial Chemistry to give help to those branches of the chemical industry most closely allied to the Salters' old occupation. The Institute at first gave help to men whose university careers had been interrupted by the war. Now Salters' fellowships are available for post-graduate research in chemistry, chemical engineering and chemical technology and for school science masters to enable them to spend a sabbatical term in a university department of chemical engineering. The Salters' Institute also promotes a yearly conference for school teachers at a university. Because the Company's choice of the way in which it can help its old trade is unhampered by narrow traditions, it is not afraid to adopt new schemes and discard them if after all they do not serve a useful purpose.

Not every Company is in a sufficiently robust financial position to endow a university college or to found a technical school, but this does not prevent them trying to regenerate interest in their old crafts. They cannot fill up the ranks with practising craftsmen, as the number of those prepared to learn a trade the hard way is dwindling rapidly. Two to five years spent apprenticed to a master craftsman seems a poor alternative to the carefree life of a student at a technical college, and the amount of work which can now be performed by sophisticated machinery discourages people from learning a craft. Yet in shoeing a horse, making a barrel or staining glass no amount of theory can make up for first-hand experience. So Companies who represent dying crafts are worried about the shortage of skilled craftsmen. The craft of the cooper has been dwindling since beer was produced in metal containers, and in 1970 the last cooper's apprentice was rolled out in a barrel to mark his promotion from apprentice to journeyman cooper. This is the messy but traditional treatment of 'Truss O' reserved by coopers for apprentices when they finish their time. The poor lad is tossed into a barrel which has been filled with the most appalling mixture of well-watered muck, rolled in it over the uneven cobbles of the cooperage, taken out and shaken in a blanket before being declared well and truly trussed. Although there are no more apprentices on their books the Coopers Company encourages standards in its craft by presenting certificates and the freedom of the Company to those who can make a barrel well enough to satisfy the exacting standards of the craft test.

The Glaziers create a demand for craftsmen in their trade by the work they do to preserve stained glass of exceptional merit and the commissioning of fresh works of art in glass. It is not a rich Company but under a trust established in 1966 'for the

benefit of the public knowledge, understanding and appreciation of the art of stained, etched and other forms of decorative glass and glass mosaics', it has been able to preserve Pre-Raphaelite windows from condemned parish churches and come to the rescue of some valuable fifteenth-century stained glass which would otherwise have been left to disintegrate through lack of funds for restoration.

Other Companies seek to replace the discipline of the apprenticeship system with registration. The Farriers have been examining and registering shoeing smiths since the First World War and their Registration Committee consists of representatives from agriculture, the trade and the veterinary profession.

Sampling a silver chain in the Assay Office in Goldsmiths Hall. No ware is hall-marked until a sample of it has been submitted to accurate chemical analysis. The law requires that gold and silver plate shall not be sold until it has been hall-marked, and that manufacturers and importers of plate, shall bring their goods to an assay office to be assayed and if found up to standard, marked with the prescribed marks for gold of 22, 18, 14 or 9 carats, or for Britannia (.958) silver or sterling (.925) as the case may require.

The Company also encourages high standards in its craft by presenting medals for good shoeing at agricultural shows around the country. The Plumbers in 1884 established a register for those plumbers who had satisfied the Company as to their capabilities. To help the public in their search for good workmanship any plumber who is so registered may use the letters RP after his name. The Company has spent many thousands of pounds trying to make its registration a compulsory qualification for all plumbers, but so far has failed to make it a statutory necessity.

The Stationers Company had been registering literary secrets and copyright for over three hundred years, until in 1911 the law relating to copyright was changed and it ceased to be necessary for authors and printers to enter their books at Stationers Hall. Nevertheless people do still voluntarily enter their creative efforts at Stationers Hall, which can be useful should a question of copyright arise. The Stationers' Copyright Registers make fascinating reading and contain some very famous names. Three of the most outstanding entries are the First Folio Shakespeare, 1623, Milton's *Paradise Lost*, 1667 and Dr Johnson's *Dictionary*, 1755. Another interesting exhibit at the hall is the 'Wicked Bible', printed by Robert Barker, a Master of the Company in the seventeenth century, who received the patent to print English Bibles and was the printer of the Authorized Version in 1611. Unfortunately the good Barker failed to spot a printer's error in one biblical edition, whereby the word 'not' was omitted from the Seventh Commandment. This carelessness with God's word led him to the Star Chamber where he was tried and heavily fined for inadvertently exhorting people to commit adultery.

Although the exercise of their powers of search would be impracticable for most Companies today, they try to encourage high standards by rewarding good work instead of condemning bad. The Saddlers still exercise their right of search over all saddles made within a two-mile radius of the City, but the majority of Companies would not dare to condemn poor quality stock for fear of legal repercussions. There are many different ways, however, in which a Company can provide a carrot for the pursuit of excellence, and prizes, medals, scholarships and bursaries are liberally dispensed. The Blacksmiths instituted their own hall-marking scheme in 1960, whereby they stamp with the Company's crest any 'fine examples of blacksmithry'. Some Companies stage exhibitions or initiate competitions. In 1882 the Horners, for instance, staged a great exhibition of horn work at the Mansion House and the Shipwrights have had three exhibitions of model sailing and steamships, tugs, fishing smacks, and apparatus connected with the operation of ships and the saving of life at sea. The City is a more attractive place as a result of the competitions run by the Gardeners Company. In London hospitals, almshouses and commercial buildings window boxes and gardens are the more vigorously tended in the hope of winning one of the Gardeners' awards. To show all these competitors how it should be done the Company has its own garden which they design and restock annually, around the Wren Church of St Dunstan in the East near the Tower. The Needlemakers and Gold and Silver Wyre Drawers visit factories in the midlands making needles and gold braid respectively. The Founders Company liverymen and Court make an annual foundry tour, which has taken them to foundries all over Europe as well as in the British Isles. The Butchers have ninety per cent of their members directly involved in the meat trade and Butchers Hall on the fringes of Smithfield market is a natural centre for trade activity. Companies like the Brewers, the Solicitors, the Master Mariners, the Furniture Makers and the Distillers are entirely composed of members of their respective trades, and get very involved with trade matters. In the case of the Brewers membership of the Court is limited to directors of brewing firms within a two and a half mile radius of London and they negotiate wages and conditions for brewery workers in London.

Blacksmiths' parcel-gilt staffhead dated 1659. It is inscribed, 'By hammer and hand, all arts doe stand.'

Active participation is more difficult for Companies who are left representing a dead or dying craft. The Bowyers and the Fletchers have found an outlet in the encouragement of archery and they sponsor competitions at meetings of the Royal Toxophilite Society. There is not much scope for deadly dalliance with a fan in the dark of a discotheque and demand for coaches is hardly pressing, so in order not to be left high and dry without a trade to support, Companies whose craft is becoming extinct have embraced the modern equivalent. The Fanmakers support the heating and ventilation trade, the Coachmakers and Harnessmakers the motor and aircraft industries, the Turners engineering, the Paviors highway construction, the Horners support the plastics industry and the Pattenmakers the manufacturers of galoshes and rubber footwear. New trades and professions have sprung up this century and given birth to robust new guilds based on the old principles, for instance, the Scientific Instrument Makers and the Guild of Air Pilots and Air Navigators.

It seems extraordinary that airmen, who are not thought to be particularly sentimental or traditional, should choose as a professional organization something so medieval as a Livery Company. The Guild of Air Pilots and Air Navigators is the nearest thing to the true craft guild and it says much for the adaptability of the system that it should still be relevant in the twentieth century. There are 300 liverymen and 1,400 freemen of the guild, all of whom must hold or have held a pilot's or a navigator's licence. The work of their Company is concerned with every aspect of flying and the aircraft industry, with its main object the highest possible standard of safety in the air. Rather like the Goldsmiths Company the Guild of Air Pilots have plenty of experts on their livery to man their various working committees. From the private buccaneer to the respectable British Airways man, their members can speak for every variety of interest within the industry. Consequently they play an important part as objective advisers between regulatory authorities and the government. The sort of problems they assist with includes, for instance, the question of introducing a cockpit voice-recorder which can record everything said in the cockpit from 'start up' to 'engines off'. Such a recording would add valuable information to that of the black box when trying to determine the cause of a crash. It would also be a great intrusion upon the pilots' privacy, as not all that is said on an eight-hour flight is always strictly concerned with flying the aircraft! For this reason the idea has encountered opposition and the guild is trying to pour oil on troubled waters by suggesting that these voice-recorders could be erased automatically on successful completion of every flight and only used in the event of something going wrong.

The guild differs from its fourteenth-century prototypes in that it has nothing to do with wages and prices and the Company tries to keep aloof from the squabble about what goes into a weekly wage packet. Consequently it has managed to earn respect for its views in government ministries and airline boardrooms, and uses these good relations to achieve for its members improvements in working conditions which might in the long run be worth more than an extra thousand pounds a year. Another way in which the Air Pilots differ is in the style of their entertaining. Although they lack an impressive hall in which to hold their dinners, and cannot hope to match the glittering array of sixteenth- and seventeenth-century silver some of the older Companies can produce on special occasions, they do entertain with a twentieth-century panache in keeping with their trade. Flying makes nothing of distances and so the Air Pilots whisk their guests off in an aeroplane for a banquet in Brussels or a medieval feast in a far-off ancient castle in Limerick. The Master even thinks nothing of flying to Melbourne for dinner with their Australian branch.

Trade was the activity which brought the guilds to power in the fourteenth and fifteenth centuries, although it was not the prime mover of the early religious fraternities from which they sprang. Social and charitable work was their first concern and

Master's Crown of the Girdlers Company believed to date from the 16th Century used in the Company's Coronation ceremony until Election day 1940. Although new crowns are used this one was recovered as a charred relic from the smoking ruins of Girdlers Hall in 1940. It was nearly fully restored and built up again and now survives as a museum piece.

it was to this role that the guilds reverted when they lost control of their trade in the eighteenth and nineteenth centuries. Then the technological needs of the present century once again made them take a more active part in trade matters. This repetitive pattern has been woven by the guilds' survival technique, by which they have maintained unbroken continuity for five to six centuries. What shape it will take next is hard to predict, for it is very difficult to make sufficient allowance for the permanency of a Livery Company. Decisions which may seem right in the present decade and for the foreseeable future could be proved wrong by the inevitable march of progress. Property for instance is particularly prone to change; schools, almshouses, halls and offices are all subject to decay, investments to crises of confidence. In preserving their Company's inheritance each generation of liverymen has to decide what is for the best in the contemporary climate. Their judgement is limited by the perspective of their age, but a Livery Company's perspective is infinite.

Index

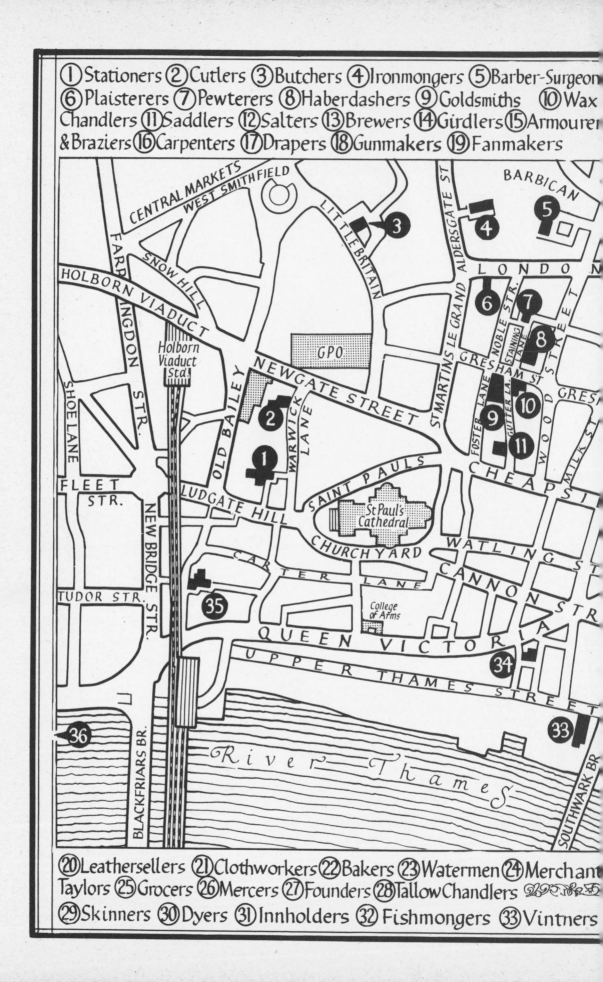

① Stationers ② Cutlers ③ Butchers ④ Ironmongers ⑤ Barber-Surgeon ⑥ Plaisterers ⑦ Pewterers ⑧ Haberdashers ⑨ Goldsmiths ⑩ Wax Chandlers ⑪ Saddlers ⑫ Salters ⑬ Brewers ⑭ Girdlers ⑮ Armourer & Braziers ⑯ Carpenters ⑰ Drapers ⑱ Gunmakers ⑲ Fanmakers

⑳ Leathersellers ㉑ Clothworkers ㉒ Bakers ㉓ Watermen ㉔ Merchant Taylors ㉕ Grocers ㉖ Mercers ㉗ Founders ㉘ Tallow Chandlers ㉙ Skinners ㉚ Dyers ㉛ Innholders ㉜ Fishmongers ㉝ Vintners